the DESIGNER'S EYEWEAR

Vision Through the Lenses of the Spiritual Gifts

SONYA G. RICHARDSON

REVISED EDITION

Editor: Kevin Miller
Photographer: Tim Horbus Photography
Cover Designer: Anointing Productions

Published and distributed in the United States by
Dior Productions

ISBN: 978-1-7360068-2-5

SHARPEN YOUR SPIRITUAL VISION

Sign up here to learn more about our eye-opening giveaways:

https://www.sonyarichardson.com/contact

Free spiritual gift assessments, books, journals, and more!

Enter your name, email address, type "Giveaway" in the message box, and submit

TABLE OF CONTENTS

Acknowledgments

Writing this book has been more rewarding than I could have ever imagined. My goal was to present a book where God's Word would resonate louder than opinions and judgments of humankind. I especially want to thank the individuals that contributed to this effort.

This would not have been possible without the unrelenting support of my husband, Gilbert G. Richardson, Sr. I am eternally grateful to Gilbert for offering theological insight, doctrinal clarification, and practical suggestions, from the book's inception to its very end. In addition, he has faithfully supported my craft and voluntarily assumed the role of my personal sounding board. Gilbert's pastoral duties and other ministerial demands did not restrict him from accommodating my writings. This unwavering support is a true testament of my husband's godly character. Thank you.

I am extremely grateful to my four talented children for collectively providing constructive advice, editorial assistance, and ongoing support in bringing my work to life. Thank you, Kiersten, Jasmine, Haley, and Gilbert Jr. It is because of your unparalleled support that I have a legacy to pass on to our family.

I would like to extend my deepest gratitude to my mother, a retired English instructor, for engaging in this writing venture, reading initial drafts, and providing content editing. I am indebted to my parents, Mack and Hilda Guillory, the first to introduce me to Christ's teachings. My upbringing as a pastor's child was shaped by godly instruction, discipline, and structure. My parents consistently modeled integrity, ethical and moral behavior, and so much more that has contributed to my journey as an author. Thanks, Dad and Mom.

An incredibly special thanks to my dear friend, Emma Robinson. I could not have asked for a more devoted accountability partner. Emma has consistently motivated and inspired me throughout this process. I am forever grateful to her for encouraging me during my occasional periods of writing inactivity. Emma has shared in every disappointment as well as every triumph that I have experienced along this writing journey. Thank you.

There are numerous others to properly thank, but I feel indebted to these individuals for their special contributions in this effort.

Introduction

I was mesmerized as I was fitted for my first pair of designer eyeglasses at my local vision center. As the eye technician displayed the large selection of new arrivals, my heart began to flutter. With a huge variety of trendy frames to choose from, I was inspired by classic styles from various designers. The office staff told me that they worked directly with top eyewear brands to create the richest, most diverse selection of designer eyewear. In addition, they reassured me that my prescriptive lenses would be precise, accurate, shatter-proof, and impact-resistant. After all, a fashionable pair of frames alone would not promote optimum vision. The designer eyewear would only become functional once the frames were fitted with the correct prescription.

When the new eyeglasses arrived for pickup, I anxiously tried them on. I was fascinated by the sharp and refreshing view through the new lenses. Not only did I achieve a fashionable look, my vision was remarkably enhanced, maximizing my ability to focus. I could now see objects close up and at a distance, which was a win-win. However, as dazzling as this experience was, it could never overshadow the moment when I was fitted for the Ultimate Designer's eyewear—my spiritual gifts.

Romans 12:6 (NLT) declares, "In his grace, God has given us different gifts for doing certain things well." When I accepted Jesus as my Lord and Savior, the Holy Spirit endowed me with a dominant spiritual gift (and other subordinate gifts), divine impartations that equipped me for service in the body of Christ, the Christian church. I was fashionably graced by God, the Ultimate Designer, through the Holy Spirit, to receive my exclusive spiritual eyewear, my assigned spiritual gifts.

During my early childhood years, I sensed the presence of these gifts as they took root and began to germinate. Over time, I prayerfully nurtured and cultivated the gifts of teaching, encouragement, and leadership. I was fitted for the Designer's ultimate eyewear, equipped to assist my local church in executing its mission. What a remarkable experience it was to receive such a rich selection. This provision, however, is not reserved exclusively for me but for all who profess Jesus Christ as their personal Lord and Savior.

Each believer receives at least one spiritual gift at the time of salvation, a specialized tool through which God works to help the church execute its mission on earth. These gifts equip members of the body of Christ to play an essential role in their local churches. This book is based on the premise that all believers should discover their spiritual gifts (1 Cor. 14:1), cultivate them, and operate in their giftedness (1 Pet. 4:10–11; 1 Cor. 12 and 14). Spiritual gifts are derivatives of the grace or favor that God bestows upon every believer.

The apostle Paul challenged the Roman Christians to use their spiritual gifts in Romans 12:4–8 (NIV).

> For just as each of us has one body with many members, and these members do not all have the same function, so in Christ we, though many, form one body, and each member belongs to all the others. We have different gifts, according to the grace given to each of us. If your gift is prophesying, then prophesy in accordance with your faith; if it is serving, then serve; if it is teaching, then teach; if it is to encourage, then give encouragement; if it is giving, then give generously; if it is to lead, do it diligently; if it is to show mercy, do it cheerfully.

The Designer's Eyewear points to God, the Ultimate Designer of an exclusive brand of spiritual eyewear, herein referred to as the "seven motivational spiritual gifts." This analogy parallels the design of physical eyewear, where each lens or gift is unique, customized, and set apart. According to 1 Corinthians 12:11, the Designer relies upon His own discretion in assigning spiritual gifts. He has predetermined which eyewear will be assigned to whom. It is not our choice but His. The Designer operates with precision and accuracy when creating the perfect spiritual eyewear. He offers a variety of styles in the form of seven fashionable gifts, the spiritual gifts of Romans 12, namely: prophecy, serving, teaching, encouragement (exhortation), giving, leadership, and mercy giving, as referenced in the preceding scriptures.

The Designer is dedicated to selecting specialized eyewear, created exclusively for believers, those who have accepted Jesus as their Lord and Savior. He offers the richest and most diverse selection of spiritual gifts, according to 1 Corinthians 12:4, "Now there are diversities (varieties) of gifts, but the same Spirit." The Designer's brand is unmatchable, incapable of being rivaled. As members of the Christian church, we trust Him to assign to each of us a supernatural gift. Again, in 1 Corinthians 14:1, the apostle Paul encouraged the church members in Corinth to earnestly desire the spiritual gifts. Believers have the option to request certain spiritual gifts, but ultimately, the Designer makes the final determination.

The motivational spiritual gifts are extensions of the Designer's grace and are not to be confused with natural talents or skills. Whereas a natural talent is the ability to perform certain physical or mental tasks well, a spiritual gift is the ability to perform certain spiritual tasks well. Natural talents are derived from natural birth, whereas spiritual gifts are derived from spiritual birth or rebirth. In addition, natural talents benefit humankind on a physical or intellectual level while spiritual gifts benefit humankind on a spiritual level. However, both talents and spiritual gifts must be recognized, developed, and exercised.

Common examples of natural talents include singing, sewing, speaking, cooking, writing, carpentry, mechanics, design, and artistic skills. Talents are often the channels through which spiritual gifts flow. For example, an artistic teenager, skilled in graphic design, who passionately creates logos and other images for the youth ministry may possess the gift of service. In addition, a talented writer who is gifted in leadership may greatly enhance his or her role as leader by crafting well-written plans. Lastly, a young millennial, a gifted giver who facilitates her local church's financial empowerment sessions, may rely on her exceptional mathematics computational skills. Although different in their derivations, talents and spiritual gifts eventually intersect.

Consider the following question: "Should new prescriptive lenses be placed into old frames?" The vast majority trained in optical care would say no because old frames may become brittle and break when the new lenses are inserted. If you place expensive lenses that you expect to last for a long time into old frames, you risk breaking the old frames and subsequently losing the new lenses. What a waste! Comparatively, a Spirit-generated gift cannot operate effectively in a weak and carnal frame characterized by a person who exhibits fleshly desires and passions and leans toward a human rather than a spiritual appetite. Once we accept Jesus as Lord of our lives, we become new creations (2 Cor. 5:17). Our old ways pass away, and the new emerges. The regenerated person's understanding is enlightened, and he or she has a new perception. New spiritual lenses (spiritual gifts) are shatter-proof and impact-resistant once they are placed into new frames, symbolic of the new person in Christ.

When each member of the local church body receives and wears his or her specialized lenses, the collective impact is explosive. Romans 12:5 reminds us that each gift is dependent on the others. Similarly, we who are many in the body of Christ are also dependent on each other. God works through the spiritual gifts, both individually and collectively, to help local churches grow and remain spiritually healthy. By God's grace, prophets warn believers of sin. Servers guard against slothfulness. Teachers steer us clear of heresy. Encouragers (exhorters) watch out for hopelessness. Givers stand against selfishness. Leaders ward off chaos. Mercy-givers demonstrate God's tender love.[1] All seven of these gifts are interdependent and comprise the Designer's specialized and exclusive eyewear.

The Designer's Eyewear serves as a useful resource to believers who have not yet discovered their spiritual gift(s). This book provides details about the attributes associated with each of the seven motivational gifts. Prayerfully read through each chapter to identify which gift best matches your spiritual purpose. You may identify with several features from the various chapters, but usually one chapter's contents will stand out above the others in terms of describing you. In addition, you will gain an understanding of the motivational tendencies that drive your behavior as well as the behavior of others. While numerous assessments, tools, and resources have been designed to help people discover their spiritual gift(s), the ultimate validation of the gifts is from the Holy Spirit, the Designer Himself. God, through His Spirit,

---

1 For more on this, see the Institute in Basic Life Principles (www.iblp.org).

confirms and validates spiritual gifts through the studying of the Bible and through confirmation from other believers.

These behaviors characterize each gifting:

- Believers gifted in *prophecy* are not rude but passionate when articulating truth.

- People gifted in *serving* do not steal the spotlight but serve with an eagerness that may be viewed as such.

- Believers gifted in *teaching* who appear to be authoritative or domineering may simply feel confident in establishing biblical truth.

- People gifted in *encouragement* who offer unsolicited advice are passionate about assisting others in resolving personal issues.

- Believers gifted in *giving* who appear to pressure others to contribute simply desire to motivate fellow Christians to glorify God by donating.

- Individuals gifted in *leadership* who are perceived as cliquish tend to gravitate toward dedicated, loyal believers who share their philosophy of ministry

- People gifted in *mercy* who appear to be weak or spineless are instead endowed with divine sensitivity.

An awareness and understanding of these motivations and tendencies will help to eliminate judgmental and condemnatory attitudes toward others with different giftings as we endeavor to serve harmoniously in the body of Christ to edify each other.

Each chapter is comprised of the following sections:

- Introduction

- Gift Overview

- New Testament References

- Motivational Tendencies

- 3 *C*'s—Characteristics, Challenges, and Choices

- Vision Enhancement

- Vision Maintenance

- The Gifted Believer's Prayer

As you read this book, select a comprehensive approach, reading all seven chapters collectively as a series, or read the chapters independently. Each chapter is designed to be read as a stand-alone piece. As you read, seek the Lord with a prayerful attitude to discover the unique eyewear He has designed just for you.

ism

CHAPTER 1

THROUGH THE LENSES OF PROPHECY

> "IF YOUR GIFT IS PROPHESYING, THEN PROPHESY
> IN ACCORDANCE WITH YOUR FAITH."
> ~ ROMANS 12:6 (NIV)

Just as prescriptive lenses improve physical vision, the motivational spiritual gifts of Romans 12 enhance our spiritual vision. Each gift functions like a pair of lenses, sharpening our spiritual focus as we serve others in the body of Christ. These gifts are frequently cited as "motivational gifts" because they are practical in nature and describe the inner motivations of gifted believers. Each believer has inherent motivational tendencies that drive the way he or she responds to various circumstances. The spiritual gifts affect how we see life and respond to the needs around us. As the Ultimate Designer, the Holy Spirit infuses each of us with a customized spiritual gift, which allows us to see people and circumstances through a specific set of lenses that remedy our impaired vision.

The Designer's Eyewear promotes godly and righteous living as a prerequisite for operating in the seven areas of spiritual giftedness. In the prelude to Romans 12, the apostle Paul urged the church in Rome to present their bodies as living sacrifices (12:1–2). He went on to urge them to offer humble service in the body of Christ (12:3). In addition, regenerated believers will also possess the fruit of the Spirit of Galatians 5:22–23—love, joy, peace, longsuffering, gentleness, goodness, faith, meekness, and temperance. Accordingly, as Spirit-filled believers wear the Designer's prescriptive lenses or spiritual eyewear, their vision will align more closely with how God views the world.

This book is based on the presumption that love conquers all. Immediately following the list of spiritual gifts, the apostle Paul further challenged the church to translate love into action (Rom. 12:9–21). He emphasized the sincerity, devotion, zeal, fervor, joy, compassion, and empathy demonstrated through genuine love. True disciples of Christ will exhibit love when operating in their spiritual giftedness. The supremacy of love always overrules the desire to disrupt the flow of the church's mission. We should never allow spiritual giftings to supersede Christian character. On the contrary, character should rise to the forefront while the gifting lags slightly. It is futile to attempt to exercise a spiritual gift without blending it with genuine affection and consideration of others. The apostle Paul eloquently expresses this spiritual truth in 1 Corinthians 13:1 (NIV): "If I speak in the tongues of men and angels, but do not have love, I am only a resounding gong or a clanging cymbal." *The Designer's Eyewear* is written with the notion that each spiritual gift is implemented and aligned with God's Word.

Gift Overview

The Ultimate Designer, God Almighty, is dedicated to presenting various exclusive options in designer eyewear just for you. In this chapter, I present one of the seven options, the first motivational spiritual gift of Romans 12, the gift of prophecy. As with the other spiritual gifts, the Holy Spirit assigns this gift to certain believers. It is a divine impartation where God's Spirit infuses individuals with a message directed to the body of believers. This gift involves speaking forth a revelation received spontaneously from God. It is a supernatural message, where the Holy Spirit injects gifted believers' minds with spiritual insight relevant for the hearers at a specific moment. Once this insight is perceived, the gifted person communicates it, as directed by the Holy Spirit. The Holy Spirit gives certain people the gift of prophecy to bring edification, exhortation (encouragement), and comfort to the hearers, according to 1 Corinthians 14:3.

In the first portion of Romans 12:6, NIV, the apostle Paul declares, "We have different gifts, according to the grace given to each of us." Just as the natural body has various members that do not perform the same functions, so it is with our spiritual nature. We are individually assigned different gifts by the same Spirit to use for God's glory and for the good of His church and His people (1 Cor. 12:11, NIV). As Paul presents these seven spiritual endowments, he says these gifts are direct products of the grace or favor that God bestows upon every believer. Spiritual gifts flow from God's grace, and Paul points out that our natural capacities are enhanced by the igniting Spirit of Christ; therefore, all believers are charged to embrace and operate in their giftedness.

Believers who have received the gift of prophecy are instructed to prophesy in accordance with their faith. Since our faith is the gauge that determines our capacity to prophesy, we will operate in increased favor as we exercise unwavering faith. We will have as much as we desire and as much as we can contain. This is what Paul means when he encourages gifted believers to release prophetic utterances in accordance with their faith. The walls of our hearts are like elastic, and our sincere desire to serve in our gifts expands them. There is no limit to our spiritual effectiveness as we use our faith as a springboard to bring edification, encouragement, and comfort to the body of Christ. The gift of prophecy is a blessing to the church and should not be quenched. This is further declared in 1 Thessalonians 5:20, where the apostle Paul gives a stern warning that prophecy is not to be ignored or despised.

The prophetic utterances spoken by believers gifted in prophecy contrasts significantly with the utterances voiced by the Old Testament prophets, who spoke the authoritative Word of God directly. The words from these prophets were recorded as scripture as they proclaimed, "Thus says the Lord," whereas the messages from those with the spiritual gift of prophecy must be tested (1 Cor. 14:29–33, KJV; 1 Thess. 5:20–21, KJV; 1 Jn. 4:1–3, KJV).

There are many misconceptions about the gift of prophecy. Let us examine a few.

- The gift of prophecy is identical to the ministry calling of a prophet.

- The scope of prophecy is limited to the prediction of the future.

- The gift of prophecy is exalted above scripture.

- New Testament prophecy is coequal to preaching or teaching.

The gift of prophecy is not to be confused with the ministry calling of a prophet. While the spiritual gift of prophecy involves speaking forth a revelation received from God, the prophetic ministry calling of a prophet is one of the leadership designations named in Ephesians 4:11, where prophesying is the dominant feature of the prophet's ministry. Such a prophet continually speaks forth revelations received from God. This calling is further validated by the frequency and accuracy by which the prophet communicates such revelations.

This ministry leadership type is designed to "equip the saints for the work of the ministry" (Eph. 4:11–12). While all believers will prophesy at some time during their service to the Lord, not all are endowed with the spiritual gift of prophecy (1 Cor. 12). Those equipped with this motivational gift will hear from the Lord more frequently, though not all people who received this gift are called to the prophetic ministry. This is true of the calling of a prophet listed in Ephesians, which says: (1) their ministry is dominated by the prophetic, (2) their office is a leadership position in the body of Christ, and (3) they are often involved in a preaching ministry.

A popular misconception is that prophecy is limited to something exclusively predictive of the future. On the contrary, this gift is not always predictive. It does not merely involve foretelling the future. Instead, to a greater degree, it involves "forthtelling" God's truth. Believers gifted in prophecy communicate truth and warn people of their accountability to God and of the impending consequences of their actions. This truth may apply to the past, present, or future.

There are those who exalt prophecy above scripture. We must guard against such misconceptions. While the gift of prophecy is valid for today, it does not supersede the authority of scripture. Prophecy is a Spirit-prompted message that must be validated by scripture. We must understand that the Bible, the unadulterated Word of God, the Holy Writ, overrides any prophetic insight or impartation. The spontaneous revelatory words of prophecy are under scripture, informed by scripture, and validated by scripture.

Some have mistakenly equated New Testament prophecy with preaching or teaching. In view of extensive misconceptions associated with this spiritual gift, believers must rely on biblical evidence. Paul declares that all prophecy is based on a revelation (1 Cor. 13:2; 14:30). Here, the use of the noun "revelation" or the verb "to reveal" reflects divine disclosure or unveiling in which the Spirit makes known something previously hidden (Matt. 11:27; 16:17; 1 Cor. 2:10; Eph. 1:17; Phil. 3:15). Thus, prophecy is not based on a hunch, supposition, inference, educated guess, or even sanctified wisdom. Prophecy is a human report of a divine revelation, a message directly from the heart of God. This is what distinguishes prophecy from preaching and teaching. Sermons and biblical instruction are always grounded in an inspired text of scripture. Prophecy, on the other hand, is based on a spontaneous revelation. Thus, Paul distinguishes between coming to the corporate meeting of the church with a "word of instruction," preaching, or teaching and coming with a "revelation" or prophecy (1 Cor. 14:26). Both are necessary components that God has ordained for the local body.

As Christians, we are not to embrace messages from all who profess to be gifted in prophecy. Some have been known to misuse this powerful spiritual gift, focusing attention on themselves rather than God. Others make wild claims that tend to mislead or misguide the body of Christ. It is not God's will to arouse people with fear or confusion triggered by manipulation or the perception of danger. Beware of those who operate under such false presumptions. The gift of prophecy does not function to berate or browbeat individuals. Instead, according to 1 Corinthians 14:3, the ministry of prophecy edifies (builds up), exhorts (encourages), and comforts (consoles) believers to awaken their faith.

- *Edifies*—As hearers receive a prophetic word, they are edified, strengthened, or built up in the Lord. The Spirit-prompted message is never intended to tear people down.

- *Exhorts*—As hearers receive a prophetic word, they are also exhorted or encouraged in the Lord. A word of prophecy motivates and inspires hearers. The Spirit-prompted message is never intended to cast discouragement upon others.

- *Comforts*—As hearers receive a prophetic word, they are also comforted or consoled. Spirit-prompted utterances are meant to bring consolation and strength for the journey ahead.

In addition to the benefits that prophecy offers to believers, it also benefits non-believers. It may bring conviction of sin to non-believers who happen to be visiting the gathering of God's people as the secrets of their hearts are disclosed (1 Cor. 14: 24–25). Because of this spiritual encounter, outsiders will be moved to worship God and to acknowledge and declare God's presence in the setting. This can be a transformational encounter.

How was New Testament prophecy regulated during worship settings? In 1 Corinthians 14, the apostle Paul provides guidance for orderly worship. He gives instructions for exercising the gift of prophecy during the gathering of believers. The entire gathering should not be focused primarily on the operation of spiritual gifts. After all, the Creator is the object of worship, so the gifts of the Spirit should never be the primary focus. In verses 29–32, Paul declares that prophecy must be regulated within the meeting. God is not the author of confusion or chaos but of peace.

Paul further advises that only two or three prophets should speak at any given time (v. 27). In the first-century church, all believers were active participants. When the saints of Paul's day came together in worship, each person, according to 1 Corinthians 14:26, was expected to participate. While some spontaneously sang hymns, others brought forth teachings, spoke in tongues, uttered revelations, and provided interpretations. Paul steers these saints away from chaotic, disorderly services. They were not restricted, as most contemporary churches are, to a printed program; therefore, they thought it necessary to provide guidance for worship participation to achieve maximum spiritual benefit for everyone present. He reminds us in verse 26 of our objective in worship—to edify or to build up and strengthen the body of believers. He wanted to ensure that prophecy was conducted in an orderly manner. To eliminate mass confusion that could possibly erupt from spontaneous or impromptu participation, Paul regulated the number of prophets that could speak at a given time.

Paul states that others should judge the prophecies, as the prophetic messages are declared. If anyone professed to have received a word from the Lord during Paul's day, the leadership present at the meeting had the biblical authority to judge that impartation. It is clear from this passage that no one should articulate a prophetic message without it first being evaluated by mature spiritual leaders. Since believers receive prophecy through revelation (verse 30), and no one is infallible, every message should be tested and examined for spiritual soundness. After all, humans, by nature, are prone to error. This fact leads us to comply with 1 John 4:1 (NIV), "Dear friends, do not believe every spirit, but test the spirits to see whether they are from God, because many false prophets have gone out into the world."

Paul envisions prophetic utterances as a teaching mechanism (1 Cor. 14:31). He also viewed these as a conduit for certain spiritual gifts to be identified and imparted (1 Tim. 4:14). Luke describes situations in which prophecy can provide divine direction for ministry (Acts 13:1–3) as well as to issue warnings to God's people (Acts 21:4, 10–14). In addition, true prophets never prophesy "on demand" but "by command" of God. If God does not impart it, neither do they.

Unrehearsed, unscripted, spontaneous participation was the norm for worship during Paul's era. The saints willingly participated in the services, sharing whatever God placed in them to share. In addition, as noted earlier, Paul ensured that the meetings were regulated by order. We have lost this sense of active engagement in our contemporary churches. Ministering with our spiritual gifts has been replaced with rigid, unbending, pre-planned, and pre-printed programs. Many congregations do not allot any space during worship for the people of God to exercise their spiritual gifts. Participation from the "regular" church members is forbidden in these settings. Instead of utilizing the program merely as a guide, it is used as an instrument to divide—

in particular, those in the pews from those on the stage. Strict adherence to church programs and bulletins isolates us from the Lord's presence during worship.

Following a pre-planned program is not inherently wrong; however, it can become a major stumbling block if it prevents us from yielding to the Holy Spirit's leading. On the other hand, in some instances, modern congregations allow participants to function in a disorderly way through the misuse and mishandling of spiritual gifts. In these settings, you may witness individuals staging wild "performances" supposedly in the name of Christ. The church's leadership is responsible for providing sound biblical instruction in all spiritual matters, including how gifts of the spirit operate in their gatherings and ministries. Whether or not your local church utilizes a pre-planned program or bulletin, worship should be conducted in an unrestricted manner, always leaving room for God's presence to saturate the meeting.

Finally, Paul's renowned call to order is echoed in 1 Corinthians 14:40 (NIV), "Let all things be done decently and in order." God established a culture wherein spiritual gifts can operate effectively. When spiritual gifts lean toward an unscriptural focus, it discredits and grieves the Holy Spirit. It may also lead others to dishonor the spiritual gifts and bypass the benefits they offer. We should always be guided by 1 Peter 4:10, which encourages us to use our gifts as faithful stewards in serving others well.

Prophecy in the New Testament

Prophetic ministry in the early church was both widespread and diverse. The following examples give us a glimpse of the workings of prophecy during this era.

- The prophet Agabus predicted a famine (Acts 11:27–29)

- The prophets Barnabas, Simeon (who was called Niger), Lucius, Manaen, and Saul, were active in the church at Antioch (Acts 13:1)

- The four daughters of Phillip the evangelist prophesied (Acts 21:8–9)

Prophecy, the gift of the Spirit designed for edifying the body of Christ, was also utilized in the following churches:

- Rome (Rom. 12:6)

- Corinth (1 Cor. 12:7–11; 14:1–40)

- Ephesus (Eph. 2:20)

- Thessalonica (1 Thess. 5:19–22)

We cannot ignore the highest prophetic voice of all times, our Lord and Savior, Jesus. While the Bible contains numerous accounts, let us consider the Lord's conversation with the Samaritan woman at Jacob's well (Jn. 4:1–42). All alone at the well (his disciples had gone into a nearby village to purchase food), Jesus encountered a Samaritan woman who had come for water. Christ overcame two cultural barriers—one gender and the other racial—by speaking in public to a non-Jewish female (vv. 9, 27). He led her gently into a conversation, intriguing her with the promise of some sort of water that could quench her thirst eternally. He established His prophetic authority by revealing details of her past that no ordinary person could have known. She hurried back to her village and spread the news of this remarkable man.[2]

---

2 Wayne Jackson, "Jesus, the Master Teacher," *Christian Courier,* last visited April 29, 2020, https://www.christiancourier.com/articles/1497–jesus-the-master-teacher.

Motivational Tendencies

The motivational gifts of Romans 12 are practical in nature and describe the inner motivations of the Christian servant. These seven gifts produce certain motivating or influencing tendencies that influence how gifted believers relate to others and to their surroundings. The Holy Spirit infuses every believer with qualities that shape their overall perspectives on life. Because of this, gifted individuals find themselves unconsciously acting out specific inherent tendencies. This is an indication of our Creator's unique craftsmanship.

Those who minister or serve in the gift of prophecy are motivated to correct sin while restoring or maintaining people's relationship with God through edification, encouragement, and consolation. Such gifted believers are moved to sound the alarm and warn others of sin and evil. They become highly frustrated and disappointed when those who profess Christ tolerate sin and compromise with the world rather than seek correction.

Are you gifted in prophecy? Do you become extremely concerned over the sins of others? Are you passionate about speaking the truth to restore people to Christ? Do people often accuse you of being too blunt or judgmental? Perhaps you have a sharp sense of right and wrong, void of any gray areas.

As you continue this journey of identifying and confirming your spiritual gift, examine whether the motivations associated with prophecy align with your decision-making and actions. If so, offer praises to our Almighty God for entrusting you with such a beautiful ornament, the gift of prophecy. If the attributes described do not reflect your motivations, I encourage you to continue seeking the Lord in the validation of your spiritual gift(s).

Let us observe what it is like to view people and circumstances through the eyes of prophecy. The following list provides common descriptions of those endowed with this spiritual gift.

- They are passionate about exposing sin so that truth can be revealed and fellowship with God can be restored.

- They are dedicated and loyal to truth even over friendship.

- For these gifted believers, any solution that involves compromise is unacceptable. They have a sense of urgency as it relates to reconciling sinners back to God.

- Those with the gift of prophecy often display the gift of discerning spirits; they can discern true motives as the Holy Spirit gives them divine insights.

- As a rule, people with the gift of prophecy are more interested in whether the heart is pure than whether the activity in question is acceptable.

- Because people with the gift of prophecy are usually bold and outspoken, their actions can easily be interpreted as rude or arrogant. Their need to be sorely truthful may sometimes result in insensitivity or harshness.

- Their sense of conviction may cause them to become intolerant or prideful. Because of this, it is imperative that they prayerfully seek the Lord for guidance in operating in the spirit of Christian love.

- Believers with the gift of prophecy bear a deep consciousness of sin, sometimes in the form of a burden. This may induce a negative or gloomy approach to life.

- Because they carry a heavy load, such gifted believers must diligently pursue spiritual, mental, and physical rejuvenation.

Do you recognize any of these traits within you? If not, then perhaps you've observed a number of these in other believers. Either way, you are now on your way to gaining further insight into the common traits associated with the gift of prophecy.

These characterizations give credence to the motivation of prophecy: to correct and restore. Individuals gifted in prophecy have a deep sense of conviction, driven by a passion to restore or maintain people's fellowship with God. Now that you've experienced what the world looks like through the lenses of prophecy, you can develop a keener appreciation for this gift as well as for those who serve in this ministry capacity.

The 3 *C's*—Characteristics, Challenges, and Choices

While each person in the body of Christ is unique, it is not unusual for those who operate in the same motivational gift to demonstrate common *characteristics*, to experience common *challenges*, and to serve in similar *choices,* or capacities in ministry.

Characteristics

While everyone in the body of Christ is unique, a believer who operates in the gift of prophecy may possess several of the following characteristics.

- Easily distraught over the sins of others

- Passionate about exposing sin to reconcile people to God

- Encourages repentance for the glory of God

- Confident in the use of scripture

- Communicates strongly what he or she perceives

- Exhibits a strong desire to obey God

- Articulates truth powerfully and persuasively

- Outspoken, direct, and sometimes blunt

- Holds to convictions and opinions

- Sees the world in black or white—doesn't work in a gray world

- Has a keen sense of right and wrong

- Recognizes character in people, whether good or bad

- Is an introvert rather than an extrovert

- Holds himself or herself and others to a high standard

- Has a strong desire to see God's plan unfold in people's lives

- Promotes spiritual growth in others

Although each person's behavior will vary according to factors such as age, gender, culture, environment, background, temperament, and experiences, it is common for those who have the motivational gift of prophecy to demonstrate the above characteristics.

Challenges

While everyone in the body of Christ is unique, a believer who operates in the gift of prophecy may encounter one or more of the following challenges.

- Judgmental, self-righteous, and blunt

- Exposes truth without restoring

- Delights in goal accomplishment rather than forward progress

- Forces others toward spiritual growth

- Engages reluctantly in healthy compromises

- Inflexible or unbending

- Critical and pessimistic

- Often interpreted as prideful or arrogant

- Does not readily exercise positive reinforcement

- Lacks tactfulness

- Impersonal or insensitive

- Intolerant of other views

- Struggles with self-image

We must recognize and acknowledge these challenges and pray diligently to overcome them. The Holy Spirit assigns spiritual gifts to equip believers to benefit others and to glorify God. These special endowments also reveal the Living God to non-believers. Our Heavenly Father strategically established a standard where spiritual gifts can operate in excellence. When gifted believers lean toward a carnal or selfish focus, Christ's ministry is compromised. This may lead others to dishonor the gifts and bypass the benefits that they provide.

Choices (Areas of Service)

While this list is not comprehensive, it can be used as a guide for directing those who are passionate about identifying and operating in their area of spiritual giftedness. The chart below provides the following: 1) suggested positions or areas of service, 2) descriptions of the positions or areas of service, 3) abilities and best personality traits for each position, and 4) the type of ministry or the specific group for whom the person is passionate about serving.[3]

> "YOUR GIFT IS GOD'S GIFT TO YOU; WHAT YOU
> DO WITH IT IS YOUR GIFT TO GOD."
> ~ UNKNOWN

---

3 Larry Gilbert and Cindy Spear, *The Big Book of Job Descriptions for Ministry* (Ventura, CA: Gospel Light: 2002).

Ministry Opportunities: Prophecy

Position	Description	Characteristics	Passionate About:
Senior Pastor	Provides spiritual leadership to members of a church; interprets biblical scripture	*Abilities:* Leadership, good communicator, preaching/teaching experience, counseling experience, experience in leading others to Christ *Personality Traits:* Expressive, dependable, discreet, courageous, confident, friendly, and compassionate	Nurturing and shepherding other believers, equipping people for ministry, saving souls and influencing the community for Christ
Associate Minister	Serves as an assistant to the senior pastor	*Abilities:* Able to serve in a supporting capacity *Personality Traits:* Dependable, discreet, friendly, compassionate, and reliable	Supporting the senior pastor and ministering to people

Evangelist	Converts others to the Christian faith, especially by public preaching	*Abilities:* Leadership, good communicator, preaching/teaching experience *Personality Traits:* Expressive, dependable, courageous, confident, and compassionate	Speaking the truth and connecting others to Christ through the gift of salvation

This chart serves as a guide in helping people with the gift of prophecy identify opportunities to serve others in the body of Christ. Here are additional choices for ministering in the gift of prophecy.

- Church planting

- Preaching

- Street evangelism

- Teaching

Other influencing factors drive a person's ability to minister, including age, level of spiritual maturity, and overall health (physical and emotional). I recommend that you collaborate with your local church leadership to develop your passions in ministry. Your spiritual advisors can assist you in selecting suitable options that are readily available within your local church.

Vision Enhancement

The motivational gifts function like a pair of eyeglasses, maximizing our spiritual vision. The gifts affect how we see life and respond to the needs around us. While prescriptive lenses correct or improve physical eyesight, these seven gifts alter or readjust spiritual sight. Like corrective lenses, as we "wear" these gifts, they serve as a remedy for impaired spiritual vision. They also influence our ability to focus on serving the body of Christ. To enhance physical vision, we must be willing to seek assistance in correcting our defective eyesight. The same is true of our spiritual vision. Consider physical nearsightedness and farsightedness. These are two common defects that can improve with proper intervention. Spiritual gifts can do the same thing for our spiritual vision.

- People who are spiritually nearsighted lack foresight and can only judge what is in front of them. Since such people are short-sighted, they cannot readily see distant images, which appear blurry. Visual accuracy is limited to only what is up close—the obvious.

- Spiritually farsighted individuals, on the other hand, can clearly see distant images, but objects that are in front of them appear blurry. Farsighted people can only judge images at a great distance.

Both visual impairments, nearsightedness and farsightedness, require prescriptive lenses for visual enhancement. It is amazing how these lenses help remedy both defects and improve overall vison. Likewise, if our spiritual eyesight is defective, we must be willing to receive the remedy that the Holy Spirit prescribes in the form of spiritual gifts.

Those who operate in the motivational gifts of the Spirit must clearly see people and circumstances through the lenses of their designated gifts. If we are to serve others in the body of Christ in an effective manner, our ability to focus on spiritual matters cannot be impaired. Believers who are spiritually nearsighted lack discretion in the things of God and cannot see the big picture. They are only capable of judging what is in front of them—the obvious. To nearsighted believers, any consideration outside of their apparent reach seems blurry. On the other hand, Christians who are spiritually farsighted tend to overlook what is directly in front of them.

In these instances, defective vision represents believers who misrepresent or abuse their spiritual gift(s), operating outside of their divine scope. Here is good news: both visual defects can be remedied. God, the Ultimate Designer, has provided corrective spiritual lenses that supersede those of any earthly optometrist.

Correcting Nearsightedness in Prophecy

Persons gifted in prophecy must be careful to avoid becoming spiritually nearsighted, lacking foresight and only judging what is right in front of them. Nearsightedness symbolizes gifted believers promoting their personal agenda or leaning toward their personal weaknesses, i.e., the challenges detailed in the previous section. He or she must not become short-sighted, only focusing on self; rather, such believers must extend their spiritual vision into the distance by seeking to strengthen, encourage, and to console their hearers. They must exercise compassion and humility while refraining from demonstrating rudeness and arrogance.

Those with the gift of prophecy may exhibit nearsightedness as they focus only on articulating an up-front message without considering the hearers' personal plights. We cannot use the same cookie-cutter approach when imparting a divine utterance. Instead, we must prayerfully tailor our approach to suit the needs of the person or group being addressed. Though it is vital that messengers declare the impartation, it is equally important that they communicate as the Holy Spirit leads. Spiritual visual accuracy should go beyond the close and obvious—nearsightedness—and extend to distant images.

People gifted in prophecy must exercise sensitivity as well as spiritual discernment as they interact with others. After all, a prophetic word should strengthen, encourage and console its hearers (1 Cor. 14:3, NIV). As we minister to others, it is vital that we model our Servant-Leader, Christ, and demonstrate compassion and humility.

While the following narrative isn't necessarily applicable to the gift of prophecy, it is centered upon Christ's overarching compassion for hurting people. In Mark 5, we witness the matchless compassion of Jesus as He encounters an unfortunate man. The Lord was in the region east of the Sea of Galilee when He met a man who was possessed by unclean spirits. This man demonstrated inexplicable behavior—wandering around unclothed, living among the tombs, cutting himself with stones, breaking his shackles, and terrorizing the community. After an exchange with these wicked demons, Jesus purged this wretched man of the tormenting spirits. This incident of deliverance portrays our Savior's tender heart. Although Jesus's intent was to cast out these demons, He also performed this deed to free the afflicted man from misery. This spiritual undertaking reveals our Savior's genuine compassion and humility. Likewise, as those gifted with prophecy articulate a divine impartation, the

Holy Spirit's enabling presence operates through them. The spontaneous revelatory words spoken by gifted believers reflect a tender and compassionate heart.

In summary, believers with the gift of prophecy must correct their defective vision, their spiritual nearsightedness. While articulating God's message, those imbued with the gift of prophecy should yield to the Holy Spirit's guidance and strive to envision the distant images that are symbolic of their personal challenges. While under the Holy Spirit's influence, those with the gift of prophecy will fashion their approach to accommodate the spiritual needs of the person or group being addressed. Though it is vital that such messengers declare the impartation, it is equally important that they exhibit compassion and humility.

Correcting Farsightedness in Prophecy

Believers gifted in prophecy must also be careful of becoming spiritually farsighted. Focusing primarily on distant images or the big picture may cause us to miss the obvious—what's directly in front of us. Here, farsightedness represents our urgent quest to transform the hearts of hearers. We may be driven only to see images in the distance—the end results—without considering what's right in front of us. Those with the gift of prophecy must never become so intense or farsighted that they miss the Holy Spirit's instructions for communicating a word from God. Such farsightedness can be corrected as believers focus on the close and obvious, exercising sensitivity in communicating God's message at that moment. Again, we cannot use the same cookie-cutter approach when imparting a divine utterance. Instead, we must prayerfully tailor our approach to suit the person or group being addressed. As we minister to others, it is vital that we demonstrate flexibility, as the Spirit leads. We must correct our defective vision, our spiritual farsightedness, and strive to envision close-up images, as well.

Vision Maintenance

Maintaining optimum spiritual vision is crucial. Once we are suitably matched to our Designer's eyewear, we must strive to keep them looking like new. Our spiritual lenses should remain free of spots and smears that can affect our focus. Spots and smears may symbolize the marring effects of our gifts if we become distracted. For example, distractions in the form of gifts that you don't possess but are attempting to operate in are like a spot or a smear. We must do whatever it takes to remove these smudges by reattaching to our God-infused spiritual gift, thereby enhancing our spiritual focus.

We must be intentional when it comes to maintaining and enhancing our visual health. The Ultimate Designer, through His Son, Jesus, set the example of how to boost spiritual vision. He engaged in spiritual disciplines such as study, meditation, prayer (solitude and silence), fasting, worship, service, and fellowship with other believers. Likewise, our spiritual vision will be enhanced as we practice the following.

- Study—read and study God's Word for guidance and direction.

- Meditate—ponder God's Word to maintain spiritual focus.

- Pray—commune with God (solitude) and listen to Him (silence).

- Fast—abstain from food or other distractors for a designated period.

- Worship—engage in private and corporate worship, which connects us to God.

- Serve—assist others compassionately, as Jesus did.

- Fellowship—interact with other believers for encouragement and to equip each other for service.

As we engage in these maintenance practices, we will achieve the Designer's fashionable look. In addition, our vision will be remarkably enhanced, and our spiritual focus will be maximized. We will see objects at any distance, for we will have been fitted with the Ultimate Designer's eyewear. While optometrists utilize digital measurements to ensure an accurate and precise prescription, the Ultimate Designer operates with a precision that is unmatchable.

Finally, the gift of prophecy is a unique adornment assigned by the Holy Spirit. Once believers receive confirmation of this gift, they will achieve clearer vision through the lens of the cross. Jesus, the Anointed One, will be their focal point and example as they exercise this spiritual gift in love and faithfulness. As they fully trust the Ultimate Designer and "wear" the lenses of prophecy, they will serve the body of Christ joyfully and effectively. The Holy Spirit has assigned the eyewear of prophecy to enhance spiritual vision by adding or subtracting focusing power to the lives of gifted believers. I have shared several guarantees that accompany this corrective remedy. The spiritual lenses of prophecy prescribed by the Holy Spirit are:

- Progressive—they enable us to see both near and far

- Shatterproof—they are reliable and unbreakable

- Impact-resistant—they withstand any opposing or colliding force

- Scratch-resistant—they cannot be scratched or damaged

In addition, the frames attached to these spiritual lenses have the following features:

- Spring-loaded—they are less likely to be bent or warped

- Silicone Nose Pads—they prevent the eyeglasses from slipping

- Straps—they firmly hold the glasses in place

Congratulations! You have experienced spiritual eyesight through the lenses of prophecy. Your knowledge and appreciation of this gift have been expanded. Since it is imperative that you identify, cultivate, and operate in your assigned gifts (1 Pet. 4:10; 1 Cor. 12 and 14), I encourage you to prayerfully confirm and validate your divine endowment. Discovering and confirming your spiritual gifts will help you remain in your ministry lane, thereby avoiding a "head-on collision."

Did you recognize and thereby confirm your prophetic gift? If so, praise the Lord for adorning you with such a precious ornament – the gift of prophecy. I encourage you to continue to seek the Lord in the cultivation and operation of your divine ability. If you need further guidance in identifying your spiritual gift, prayerfully navigate through the following chapters. Continue to review the remaining motivational gifts of the Spirit for identification and confirmation.

The Gifted Believer's Prayer:

Father, in the name of Jesus, I come into your presence with adoration and praise. I confess my sins and bind myself to godly repentance. Thank you, Lord, for infusing me with the gift of prophecy. I aim to be an excellent steward of the gifting that the Holy Spirit has assigned to me. Strengthen me, Lord, as I endeavor to overcome the challenges associated with my gift. Lead me in dedicated service as I obey your mandate to use this gift to edify, encourage, and console the body of Christ. Amen.

CHAPTER 2

THROUGH THE LENSES OF SERVING

> "IF IT IS SERVING, THEN SERVE."
> ~ ROMANS 12:7 (NIV)

Just as prescriptive lenses improve physical vision, the motivational spiritual gifts of Romans 12 enhance our spiritual vision. Each gift functions like a pair of lenses, sharpening our spiritual focus as we serve others in the body of Christ. These gifts are frequently cited as "motivational gifts" because they are practical in nature and describe the inner motivations of gifted believers. Each believer has inherent motivational tendencies that drive the way he or she responds to various circumstances. The spiritual gifts affect how we see life and respond to the needs around us. As the Ultimate Designer, the Holy Spirit infuses each of us with a customized spiritual gift, which allows us to see people and circumstances through a specific set of lenses that remedy our impaired vision.

The Designer's Eyewear promotes godly and righteous living as a prerequisite for operating in the seven areas of spiritual giftedness. In the prelude to Romans 12, the apostle Paul urged the church in Rome to present their bodies as living sacrifices (12:1–2). He went on to urge them to offer humble service in the body of Christ (12:3). In addition, regenerated believers will also possess the fruit of the Spirit of Galatians 5:22–23—love, joy, peace, longsuffering, gentleness, goodness, faith, meekness, and temperance. Accordingly, as Spirit-filled believers wear the Designer's prescriptive lenses or spiritual eyewear, their vision will align more closely with how God views the world.

This book is based on the presumption that love conquers all. Immediately following the list of spiritual gifts, the apostle Paul further challenged the church to translate love into action (Rom. 12:9–21). He emphasized the sincerity, devotion, zeal, fervor, joy, compassion, and empathy demonstrated through genuine love. True disciples of Christ will exhibit love when operating in their spiritual giftedness. The supremacy of love always overrules the desire to disrupt the flow of the church's mission. We should never allow spiritual giftings to supersede Christian character. On the contrary, character should rise to the forefront while the gifting lags slightly. It is futile to attempt to exercise a spiritual gift without blending it with genuine affection and consideration of others. The apostle Paul eloquently expresses this spiritual truth in 1 Corinthians 13:1 (NIV): "If I speak in the tongues of men and angels, but do not have love, I am only a resounding gong or a clanging cymbal." *The Designer's Eyewear* is written with the notion that each spiritual gift is implemented and aligned with God's Word.

Gift Overview

The Ultimate Designer, God Almighty, is dedicated to presenting various options and exclusives in designer eyewear just for you. In this chapter, I present the second motivational spiritual gift of Romans 12, the gift of serving. As with the other spiritual gifts, the Holy Spirit assigns this gift to certain believers. It is a supernatural endowment that allows us to demonstrate love by serving others—meeting practical needs. This is usually accomplished through tangible work. Those with the gift of serving are highly motivated doers, driven by an urgent desire to satisfy physical and spiritual needs. The Holy Spirit equips such gifted believers with a unique ability to recognize needs and respond accordingly. The Holy Spirit gives certain people the gift of serving, and they are motivated to administer hands-on assistance.

For many people, this precious adornment is one of the least desirable of the seven motivational gifts. In a world where the number of narcissists seems to be increasing, few people are willing to submit to a role that requires assisting or enabling others. Instead, numerous individuals, including Christians, have embarked on an endless quest to be exalted in a superficial manner.

There are many misconceptions about the gift of serving. Let us examine two common opinions held by many. There are believers who feel that the gift of serving is a second-rate ministry. There are also those who believe that this gift was designed exclusively for the "unskilled". Both perspectives are inaccurate and cannot be substantiated scripturally. In view of numerous misconceptions associated with the gift of serving, believers must always seek truth in the Word of God.

There are many believers who view the gift of serving as a second-rate ministry. This perpective is similar to the flawed position of some Christians during the apostle Paul's era. Paul targeted their misguided beliefs about the ranking of spiritual gifts in 1 Corinthians 12. He was usually tactful about not offending his audience; however, this dilemma threatened the effectiveness of the gospel of Christ. Paul was blunt in how he addressed the arrogance and posturing that certain members of the church in Corinth had assumed. Some members of the congregation felt, as many people do today, that certain spiritual gifts are superior to others. Not wanting them to be misinformed, Paul felt an urgent need to intervene. He reminded them, according to 1 Corinthians 12:4–5, that the same Spirit is the source of all the various gifts, ministries, and activities. All qualifications for office, as well as appointments, are determined by the Lord Jesus Christ through the Holy Spirit.

Paul expounded further on the spiritual principles of unity and diversity. Just as the members of the human body are distinct in functionality yet operate in unity, so it is with believers. Each believer possesses uniqueness in character, personality, gifts, skills, and special abilities. Consequently, God expects us to blend these together to serve Him in unity. How ironic that contemporary Christians would adopt the same faulty stance that earlier believers assumed about spiritual gifts. No spiritual gifts are inferior or superior to others. Each one is equally beneficial and profitable for ministry. The gift of serving is just as valuable as all other gifts in the eyes of our Creator. God never intended for us to create exclusive clubs consisting of spiritual "superheroes."

Another popular misconception is that the gift of service was designed for the "unskilled." God, through the Holy Spirit, is the author and dispenser of all spiritual gifts. Since our Maker is no respecter of persons, He places no such restrictions on the gifts. Serving, as with any other spiritual gift, is not confined to any classification, such as ethnicity, race, culture, economic status, age, gender, denomination, location, or social status. Servers are not people who feel they have nothing valuable to contribute to ministry, nor do they resolve to serve others as a last resort. That attitude would discredit the gift and insult the God who gives it. The range of individuals who the Holy Spirit assigns to serve in the body of Christ is as wide as our color spectrum. These gifted and "colorful" servers come from all walks of life and minister quietly but effectively in building God's kingdom. Some may serve as custodians, groundkeepers, or craftsmen while others serve as deacons, praise dancers, or directors of hospitality. The diverse members of this supporting cast work diligently to bring glory to God's name. They serve others well through their consistent, dependable, and loving deeds.

Conclusively, the gift of serving was not designed exclusively for unskilled or unqualified individuals. There are no degrading duties in ministry. As the Holy Spirit infuses believers with spiritual giftings, they become endowed with a unique skill set that enables them to minister wholeheartedly. As Henry T. Blackaby says, "The reality is that the Lord never calls the qualified; He qualifies the called."[4] Gifted servers are qualified to serve as God's Spirit converts their behavioral tendencies, natural talents, skills, and special abilities into a supernatural manifestation of greatness. As we continue to seek knowledge and clarity through scripture and prayer, the Holy Spirit will illuminate our thinking and steer us away from such misconceptions.

---

4 "Henry Blackaby Quotes," azquotes.com, last visited on July 9, 2020, https://www.azquotes.com/author/38492-Henry_Blackaby.

What a superb way to build up the body of Christ in love and unity—serving others! The Holy Spirit endows numerous believers with this gift to ensure that the church's needs are met. Churches with a heavy focus on quickly assimilating members into the fold usually target new converts. As new converts join local congregations, they are usually overflowing with enthusiasm, accompanied by a willingness to help. As the leadership entrusts them with hands-on assignments that match their maturity level, new members feel a warm sense of belonging. Even if serving is not a newcomer's calling, the act of serving may lead new believers to discover their true spiritual gifts.

Serving in the New Testament

Serving in the early church was both widespread and diverse. The following examples give us a glimpse of the workings of service to others during that era.

- Deacons were called to service (Acts 6:1–6, KJV)

- Tabitha (Dorcas) sewed for the needy (Acts 9:36, KJV)

- Martha served Jesus and others (Lk. 10:38–40; Jn. 12:1–2, KJV)

- Mary wiped Jesus's feet (Jn. 12:3, KJV)

- Phoebe served Paul and others (Rom. 16:1–2, KJV)

- Stephanas's household served believers (1 Cor. 16:15, KJV)

- Aquila and Priscilla served the church with hospitality (1 Cor. 16:19)

- Mark rejoined Paul to serve as ministerial assistant (2 Tim. 4:11, KJV)

The gift of serving is also expressed as the gift of "ministering" or "helps," in 1 Corinthians 12:28 (KJV).

As mentioned earlier, we cannot ignore the most profound Servant-Leader of all, our Lord and Savior, Jesus. His demonstration of servitude here on earth was impeccable. The entire gospel—the life, death, burial, and resurrection of Christ—reflects His countless acts of submission to God and His service to humankind. Jesus left us a blueprint for ministering, centered upon a passion to serve. The following scripture passages give us a glimpse of His servant role.

- Jesus washed his disciples' feet (Jn. 13:1–17, KJV)

- Jesus described Himself as a servant (Mk. 10:42–45; Jn. 6:38; Lk. 22:7, KJV)

- The apostle Paul described Jesus as a Servant (Phil. 2:5–8, KJV)

We all need inspiration and reinforcement while serving in the body of Christ. Even though we are not all endowed with the gift of serving, we can all serve. Whether we volunteer to assist at our local church or serve as a church employee, we need to emulate our Savior by yielding to the needs of others.

Motivational Tendencies

The seven motivational gifts of Romans 12 are practical in nature and describe the inner motivations of the Christian servant. These spiritual gifts produce certain motivating or influencing tendencies that drive how believers relate to others and to their surroundings. The Holy Spirit infuses every believer with qualities that shape their overall perspective on life. Because of this, those with the gift of serving will find themselves unconsciously acting out specific inborn tendencies. This is an indication of our Creator's unique workmanship.

People gifted in serving are motivated to satisfy a practical need. These selfless individuals do not aspire to be exalted. Instead, they prefer to serve behind the scenes. While those gifted in serving are highly enthusiastic about engaging in hands-on projects, they are usually reluctant to assume leadership roles. They willingly make up the supporting cast that empowers spiritual leaders to excel in ministry.

Have you been endowed with the gift of serving? Do you immediately begin to offer hands-on assistance without being asked? Do you find yourself helping others while neglecting your own needs? Would you rather serve than delegate responsibilities to others?

As you continue in your quest to identify and confirm your gift(s), determine whether these motivational tendencies match your own. If they do, you are already reaping the joy that comes with such a beautiful ornament—the gift of serving. If the attributes described do not reflect your motivational tendencies, I encourage you to continue seeking the Lord in the validation of your spiritual gift(s).

Let us observe what it is like to view people and circumstances through the lenses of a server. The following list provides descriptions common to those who are endowed with this gift.

- Servers are highly motivated and enthusiastic about assisting others, usually through hands-on physical work.

Unfortunately, others may mistakenly interpret their eagerness to serve as self-advancement.

- Servers are unconsciously driven to meet practical needs. As soon as servers perceive such a need, they have an irresistible urge to satisfy it.

- Servers frequently place the needs of others above their own. They have a caring and selfless nature.

- Servers have a difficult time turning others away. The inability to say "no" may result in servers overextending themselves. Consequently, a server's family or household is often neglected due to this excessive load.

- A server would rather perform a task than delegate responsibilities. In many instances, such servers may appear to be running a one-man show.

- Servers work speedily and expeditiously with efficiency as their utmost goal.

- A server's adrenalin begins to flow rapidly when a tangible need appears. It is often a challenge for non-servers to match the server's momentum. When a non-server fails to keep up, servers may view this inability as laziness.

- Servers are criticized sometimes for jumping ahead and not following protocol. They may satisfy a need without acquiring authorization or approval. This is a result of a server unconsciously operating in the "see and do" mode.

- Servers often seek approval when serving. When appreciation for the services rendered is not given, servers may become highly disappointed or saddened. These emotions should not be misinterpreted as desire for attention or grandeur. Servers perceive gratitude as a measurement of the overall effectiveness of their service.

- Servers have no desire to be in the spotlight; instead, they are contented working in the background, positioning others to achieve.

- Servers may prefer assisting in short-term assignments. Their sense of satisfaction comes from completing a task quickly and thoroughly, thereby establishing an instant record of success.

- Servers tend to be detail-oriented. The people they assist are amazed by the servers' sharp memory and knack for details. People are delighted to receive help from someone who remembers names, colors, dimensions, and other preferences.

In conclusion, a server's basic motivation is to meet practical needs. They experience ultimate fulfillment as opportunities to serve are presented. For servers, few moments are more gratifying than performing such selfless deeds. Extending their hearts to support the ministry also brings glory and honor to our Lord and Savior.

God has equipped each believer with at least one tailor-made gift that matches their purpose and destiny. Your entire personality, including your motivations and tendencies, bear the imprint of your gift. If you have the gift of service, you will see yourself in the description that follows.

3 *C's*—Characteristics, Challenges, and Choices

While each person in the body of Christ is unique, it is not unusual for those who operate in the same motivational gift to demonstrate common characteristics, to experience common challenges, and to serve in similar choices, or capacities in ministry.

Characteristics

While everyone in the body of Christ is unique, a believer who operates in the gift of serving may possess several of the following characteristics.

- A desire to meet practical needs willingly and speedily

- A hands-on approach and enjoyment from doing manual projects

- A dislike of slothfulness

- A desire to be precise and orderly, focusing on details

- A friendly, graceful, and humble personality

- Difficulty turning others away

- A greater interest in others than in self

- A preference for short-time assignments

- A preference to express him or herself through actions rather than verbal communication

- A desire for approval and appreciation

- Goes above and beyond what is asked

- Enjoys being helpful

- Has a high energy level and is highly motivated

- Prefers to perform tasks rather than delegate them

- Supports leadership and frees the leader to achieve

- Prefers to work in a supporting role

- Prefers not to be in the forefront or the public eye

- Has a natural ability to foresee obstacles while making projections and planning

- Feels inadequate or unqualified for spiritual leadership

Although each person's behavior will vary according to factors such as age, gender, culture, environment, background, temperament, and experiences, it is common for those who have the motivational gift of serving to demonstrate these characteristics.

Challenges

While everyone in the body of Christ is unique, a believer who operates in the gift of serving may encounter some of the following challenges.

- Criticizes those who are not serving

- Is saddened when unappreciated

- Works beyond physical limits

- Is impatient with those perceived as slothful

- Neglects him or herself or his or her family due to a desire to help others

- Does not want to be served by others

- Serves with an eagerness that may be viewed as self-advancement

- Has an urgency to assist that may be viewed as pushiness

We must acknowledge these challenges and pray diligently to overcome each. As we minister, God's purpose for spiritual gifts must always be at the forefront. He establishes a standard where spiritual gifts can operate in excellence. When gifted believers lean toward a carnal focus, Christ's ministry is compromised. This leads others to discredit the gifts and bypass the benefits they provide. As we stand on the pillar of Philippians 4:13, we can overcome all challenges through Christ, who gives us strength.

Choices (Areas of Service):

While this list is not comprehensive, it can be used as a guide for directing those who are passionate about identifying and operating in their area of spiritual giftedness. The chart below provides the following: 1) suggested positions or areas of service, 2) descriptions of the positions or areas of service, 3) abilities and best personality traits for each position, and 4) the type of ministry or the specific group for whom the person is passionate about serving.[5]

"YOUR GIFT IS GOD'S GIFT TO YOU; WHAT YOU DO WITH IT IS YOUR GIFT TO GOD." ~ UNKNOWN

---

5 Larry Gilbert and Cindy Spear, *The Big Book Job Descriptions for Ministry* (Ventura, CA: Gospel Light: 2002).

Ministry Opportunities: Serving

Position	Description	Characteristics	Passionate About:
Deacon or Deaconess	Responsible for ministering to the needs of church members and supporting the pastor	*Abilities:* Enjoys working with people *Personality Traits:* Dependable, compassionate discreet, good moral character	Ministering to the body of Christ Assisting the pastor with ministry work
Food Services Director	Responsible for organizing and overseeing the preparation of food	*Abilities:* Good organizational skills, leadership *Personality Traits:* Dependable, hospitable, patient	Having orderly and clean facilities to promote an efficient fellowship ministry

| Greeter | Responsible for ensuring that every person in the church is greeted and that visitors are aided as appropriate | *Abilities:* Comfortable talking to or greeting guests; able to provide good directions for church facilities

Personality Traits: Hospitable, not shy, sensitive to the needs of others, and dependable | Making people feel welcome |
| Social Media Administrator | Responsible for developing content for social media platforms | *Abilities:* Strategy planning, understanding of how content works on social media, optimizing content and technology, creative mindset, writing skills, marketing skills, organizational skills

Personality Traits: Dependable, adaptable, patient | Creating and managing content that promotes the mission and vision of the local congregation |

This chart serves as a guide in helping gifted servers identify opportunities to minister to others in the body of Christ. Here are other suggestions for serving.

- Clerical: record-keeping, word processing, telephoning

- Communications: audio-visual aids, drama, film/video-making, graphic arts, music, photography, publicity, sound system

- Hospitality: greeters, reception desk, visitation

- Service-oriented: building maintenance, custodian, cooking, landscaping, social planning, usher

Other influencing factors drive people's ability to minister, including age, level of spiritual maturity, and overall health (physical and emotional). It is highly recommended that you collaborate with your local church leadership to develop your passion in ministry. Your spiritual advisors can assist you in selecting suitable options that are readily available within your local church.

In summary, believers gifted in serving are motivated by the urgency to meet a tangible need. Now that you've seen what things look like through the lenses of serving, you can develop a deeper appreciation for this gift, whether or not you have it.

Vision Enhancement

The motivational gifts function like a pair of eyeglasses, maximizing our spiritual vision. The gifts affect how we see life and respond to the needs around us. While prescriptive lenses correct or improve physical eyesight, these seven gifts alter or readjust spiritual sight. Like corrective lenses, as we "wear" these gifts, they serve as a remedy for impaired spiritual vision. They also influence our ability to focus on serving the body of Christ. To enhance physical vision, we must be willing to seek assistance in correcting our defective eyesight. The same is true of our spiritual vision. Consider physical nearsightedness and farsightedness. These are two common defects that can improve with proper intervention. Spiritual gifts can do the same thing for our spiritual vision.

- People who are spiritually nearsighted lack foresight and can only judge what is in front of them. Since such people are short-sighted, they cannot readily see distant images, which appear blurry. Visual accuracy is limited to only what is up close—the obvious.

- Spiritually farsighted individuals, on the other hand, can clearly see distant images, but objects that are in front of them appear blurry. Farsighted people can only judge images at a great distance.

Both visual impairments, nearsightedness and farsightedness, require prescriptive lenses for visual enhancement. It is amazing how these lenses help remedy both defects and improve overall vison. Likewise, if our spiritual eyesight is defective, we must be willing to receive the remedy that the Holy Spirit prescribes in the form of spiritual gifts.

Those who operate in the motivational gifts of the Spirit must clearly see people and circumstances through the lenses of their designated gifts. If we are to serve others in the body of Christ in an effective manner, our ability to focus on spiritual matters cannot be impaired. Believers who are spiritually nearsighted lack discretion in the things of God and cannot see the big picture. They are only capable of judging what is in front of them—the obvious. To nearsighted believers, any consideration outside of their apparent reach seems blurry. On the other hand, Christians who are spiritually farsighted tend to overlook what is directly in front of them.

In these instances, defective vision represents believers who misrepresent or abuse their spiritual gift(s), operating outside of their divine scope. Here is good news: both visual defects can be remedied. God, the Ultimate Designer, has provided corrective spiritual lenses that supersede those of any earthly optometrist.

Correcting Nearsightedness in Serving

Persons gifted in serving must be careful of becoming spiritually nearsighted, lacking foresight and only judging what is in front of them. Here, nearsightedness symbolizes gifted believers promoting their personal agenda or leaning toward their personal weaknesses, i.e., the challenges detailed in the previous section. Farsightedness, on the other hand, represents a server's inability to acknowledge the needs of others. They must not become short-sighted, only focusing on self. Rather, servers must extend their spiritual vision into the distance by cheerfully aiding and supporting their local church. In addition, they must exercise patience and understanding while refraining from criticizing or belittling those who lack this gift.

Servers exhibit nearsightedness when they bend over backwards to impress leadership while disregarding the feelings of those assisting them. It is nearly impossible for non-servers to match a server's zeal, speed, and momentum. When their assistants fail to keep up, servers tend to view it as laziness.

Because of servers' strong disdain for slothfulness, they may resort to nonconstructive criticism. For example, if a server criticizes those who are not as compelled to serve, this may affect his or her ability to enlist help for future tasks. Also, this blatant disregard for others may create a contentious or hostile work environment. As a result, the server's initial intent, which was to meet a practical need, may be overridden by a destructive verbal dart. Conversely, onlookers may develop disdain for servers rather than valuing their supportive role. In this case, a deed that was intended to be spiritually fruitful becomes tainted and spiritually unfruitful.

Criticism should reflect constructive advice that expresses Christ's attributes. Our visual accuracy should go beyond the close and obvious—nearsightedness—and extend to distant images. Gaining approval from those they serve is obvious to servers, but distant images are often blurry. The gift of serving should never be blurred by the expectation of approval or appreciation from those being served. Rather, it should depict a clear vision of ministering and a focus on serving God, not people. People gifted in serving must see beyond the close and obvious, which is to receive appreciation. They must extend their vision into the distance and demonstrate appreciation. This involves cultivating a heart of pure love and exercising sensitivity. Gifted servers operating in holiness understand that their exceptional abilities are supernatural and that their assistants or helpers cannot match their capacity unless they also share this gift.

Finally, servers should aim to model our Servant-Leader, Christ, by demonstrating patience and humility. We must correct our spiritual nearsightedness and strive to envision the distant images, overcoming challenges associated with our spiritual gift(s).

Correcting Farsightedness in Serving

Servers must also be careful of becoming spiritually farsighted. Focusing primarily on distant images or the big picture may cause them to miss the obvious—what is directly in front of them. Here, farsightedness represents servers' inherent desire to meet a tangible need. They may be driven only to see images in the distance—the end results of a prestigious project—without considering what is in front of them, such as their responsibilities at home. They are desperately seeking a pat on the back or some other sign of approval for their diligent service. Instead of focusing only on the distant images or end results, those with the gift of service must also meet the demands at home. They must never become so intense or farsighted that they miss the Lord's instructions for ministering to those closest to them. This impaired vision, farsightedness, can be corrected as servers focus on the obvious, attending to their immediate family and household affairs. Servers can greatly benefit from Paul's words in 1 Timothy 3:5 (NIV), "If anyone does not know how to manage his own family, how can he take care of God's church?" In this passage, Paul was addressing those who desired a pastoral office; however, this message applies to all believers. Before attempting to minister in the local church, maintain a well-ordered household. After all, our families should reflect the body of Christ. We must correct defective vision, spiritual farsightedness, and strive to envision close-up images as well.

As disciples of Christ, we must always exhibit courtesy and kindness while exercising our spiritual gifts. The Holy Spirit enables us to minister effectively to His church with a graceful, heavenly flavor—love. The supremacy of love must always overrule our desire to offend. It is futile to attempt to exercise a spiritual gift without blending it with genuine affection and consideration of others. The apostle Paul eloquently expresses this spiritual truth in 1 Corinthians 13:1 (NIV), "If I speak in the tongues of men or of angels, but do not have love, I am only a resounding gong or a clanging cymbal."

Vision Maintenance

Maintaining optimum spiritual vision is crucial. Once we are suitably matched to our Designer's eyewear, we must strive to keep them looking like new. Our spiritual lenses should remain free of spots and smears that can affect our focus. Spots and smears may symbolize the marring effects of our gifts if we become distracted. For example, distractions in the form of gifts that you don't possess but are attempting to operate in are like a spot or a smear. We must do whatever it takes to remove these smudges by reattaching to our God-infused spiritual gift, thereby enhancing our spiritual focus.

We must be intentional when it comes to maintaining and enhancing our visual health. The Ultimate Designer, through His Son, Jesus, set the example of how to boost spiritual vision. He engaged in spiritual disciplines such as study, meditation, prayer (solitude and silence), fasting, worship, service, and fellowship with other believers. Likewise, our spiritual vision will be enhanced as we practice the following.

- Study—Read and study God's Word for guidance and direction.

- Meditate—Ponder God's Word to maintain spiritual focus.

- Pray—Commune with God (solitude) and listen to Him (silence).

- Fast—Abstain from food or other distractors for a designated period.

- Worship—Engage in private and corporate worship, which connects us to God.

- Serve—Assist others compassionately, as Jesus did.

- Fellowship—Interact with other believers for encouragement and to equip each other for service.

As we engage in these maintenance practices, we will achieve the Designer's fashionable look. In addition, our vision will be remarkably enhanced, and our spiritual focus will be maximized. We will see objects at any distance, for we will have been fitted with the Ultimate Designer's eyewear. While optometrists utilize digital measurements to ensure an accurate and precise prescription, the Ultimate Designer operates with a precision that is unmatchable.

Finally, the gift of serving is a unique adornment assigned by the Holy Spirit. Once believers receive confirmation of this gift, they will seek to achieve clearer vision through the lens of the cross. Jesus, the Anointed One, will be their focal point and example as believers exercise this spiritual gift in love and faithfulness. As they fully trust God, the Ultimate Designer, and "wear" the lenses of serving, they will minister with a touch of grace. The Holy Spirit has assigned the eyewear of serving to enhance spiritual vision by adding or subtracting focusing power to the lives of such gifted believers. I have shared several guarantees that accompany this corrective remedy. The spiritual lenses of serving prescribed by the Holy Spirit are:

- Progressive—they enable wearers to see both near and far

- Shatterproof—they are reliable and unbreakable

- Impact-resistant—they withstand any opposing or colliding force

- Scratch-resistant—they cannot be scratched or damaged

In addition, the frames attached to these spiritual lenses have the following features:

- Spring-loaded—they are less likely to be bent or warped

- Silicone Nose Pads—they prevent the eyeglasses from slipping

- Straps—they hold the glasses firmly in place

Congratulations! You have experienced spiritual eyesight through the lenses of serving. Your knowledge and appreciation of this gift have been expanded. Since it is imperative that you identify, cultivate, and operate in your assigned gifts (1 Pet. 4:10; 1 Cor. 12 and 14), I encourage you to prayerfully confirm and validate your divine endowment. Discovering and confirming your spiritual gifts will help you remain in your ministry lane, thereby avoiding a head-on collision.

Can you confirm that the act of serving others is your ministry focus? If so, praise the Lord for adorning you with such a precious ornament—the gift of serving. I encourage you to continue to seek the Lord in the cultivation and operation of your divine gift. If you need further guidance in identifying your gift, prayerfully navigate through the following chapters, and continue to review the remaining motivational gifts of the Spirit for identification and confirmation.

The Gifted Believer's Prayer:

Father, I come to you in the name of Jesus. I exalt you and make known to you my adoration and praise. Forgive my trespasses as I forgive those who have trespassed against me. Almighty God, from the fruit of my lips, I offer thanksgiving to you, for I appreciate this precious gift of serving. I treasure your Word, for it is perfect and complete. As I yield myself to your service of meeting the needs of others, empower me to overcome all distractions associated with this gift. May all that I perform in your name bring glory and honor to you.

CHAPTER 3

THROUGH THE LENSES OF TEACHING

"IF IT IS TEACHING, THEN TEACH."
~ ROMANS 12:7 (NIV)

Just as prescriptive lenses improve physical vision, the motivational spiritual gifts of Romans 12 enhance our spiritual vision. Each gift functions like a pair of lenses, sharpening our spiritual focus as we serve others in the body of Christ. These gifts are frequently cited as "motivational gifts" because they are practical in nature and describe the inner motivations of gifted believers. Each believer has inherent motivational tendencies that drive the way he or she responds to various circumstances. The spiritual gifts affect how we see life and respond to the needs around us. As the Ultimate Designer, the Holy Spirit infuses each of us with a customized spiritual gift, which allows us to see people and circumstances through a specific set of lenses that remedy our impaired vision.

The Designer's Eyewear promotes godly and righteous living as a prerequisite for operating in the seven areas of spiritual giftedness. In the prelude to Romans 12, the apostle Paul urged the church in Rome to present their bodies as living sacrifices (12:1–2). He went on to urge them to offer humble service in the body of Christ (12:3). In addition, regenerated believers will also possess the fruit of the Spirit of Galatians 5:22–23—love, joy, peace, longsuffering, gentleness, goodness, faith, meekness, and temperance. Accordingly, as Spirit-filled believers wear the Designer's prescriptive lenses or spiritual eyewear, their vision will align more closely with how God views the world.

This book is based on the presumption that love conquers all. Immediately following the list of spiritual gifts, the apostle Paul further challenged the church to translate love into action (Rom. 12:9–21). He emphasized the sincerity, devotion, zeal, fervor, joy, compassion, and empathy demonstrated through genuine love. True disciples of Christ will exhibit love when operating in their spiritual giftedness. The supremacy of love always overrules the desire to disrupt the flow of the church's mission. We should never allow spiritual giftings to supersede Christian character. On the contrary, character should rise to the forefront while the gifting lags slightly. It is futile to attempt to exercise a spiritual gift without blending it with genuine affection and consideration of others. The apostle Paul eloquently expresses this spiritual truth in 1 Corinthians 13:1 (NIV): "If I speak in the tongues of men and angels, but do not have love, I am only a resounding gong or a clanging cymbal." *The Designer's Eyewear* is written with the notion that each spiritual gift is implemented and aligned with God's Word.

Gift Overview

The Ultimate Designer, God Almighty, is dedicated to presenting various options and exclusives in designer eyewear just for you. In this chapter, I present one of the seven options, the third motivational spiritual gift of Romans 12, the gift of teaching. As with the other spiritual gifts, the Holy Spirit assigns this gift to certain believers. A gifted teacher is passionate about discovering and validating biblical truth. Those who are endowed with this gift love to study God's Word for extended periods of time. "They consume the scriptures as food for their hearts, souls and minds, with the expressed purpose of knowing Him and then making Him known to others."[6]

A believer gifted in teaching strives to achieve doctrinal integrity. The scriptures clearly illustrate how a teacher "uses sound, rational, and instructive reasoning to convince and help others to learn more about God's Word."[7] An effective teaching ministry is essential to a church's growth and survival. Sound biblical instruction serves as a guard against apostasy, a willful falling away from or an abandonment of the faith. Without gifted teachers, the local church will succumb to error. This leads to an avalanche of sinful behavior and the church's ultimate demise. As those who are gifted in teaching assume their rightful place, local churches are characterized by renewal, restoration, and revival.

Some people hold inaccurate views about the gift of teaching. Many of these are based on biased thinking and lack of understanding. There are two common misconceptions maintained by many Christians. One view is that matriculation

6 "Spiritual Gifts," *spiritualgiftstest.com,* last visited April 29, 2020, https://spiritualgiftstest.com/spiritual-gifts/.

7 "Gifts Explained," *gifttest.org,* last visited April 29, 2020, https://www.gifttest.org/gifts-explained/.

at an academic institution is a qualifier for operating in the gift of teaching. The other perspective is that any believer who strongly desires to teach God's Word should be given the opportunity. Both views are inaccurate and cannot be substantiated by scripture.

Matriculation at an academic institution does not qualify one to operate in the gift of teaching. Many people mistakenly think that college graduates, especially those with a degree in education, are equipped to be teachers of the Word. While a schoolteacher possesses academic skills that enhance learning, this is not a prerequisite for biblical instruction. Worldly knowledge without the supernatural empowerment of God's Spirit is fruitless. It is possible for an educator to present a Bible lesson that will not yield maximum spiritual results. If they have not been endowed with the gift of teaching, they cannot effectively communicate knowledge or applications of scripture. On the other hand, it is possible for a person who has no formal education to present scripture explosively. The gift of teaching is not reserved for any specific classification of believers. The Holy Spirit infuses believers from all walks of life with this special gift.

Let us not, however, diminish the effectiveness of an educator who is supernaturally gifted in teaching. The body of Christ has been tremendously impacted by this explosive combination. Numerous church groups have benefited greatly from the resulting attributes: knowledge of a subject matter, knowledge of curriculum development, systematic and clear lesson objectives, and various teaching methods and styles. In addition, these gifted individuals may employ effective disciplinary skills necessary for instructing children and teens. Educators infused with the gift of teaching have been instrumental in presenting transformational Bible lessons. These teachers "view Bible lessons and presentations primarily as an academic activity with a spiritual benefit, rather than a spiritual activity with an academic benefit."[8]

Another misconception is that any believer who has a desire to teach God's Word should be given the opportunity. This should never be the rule of thumb in our churches. When someone receives the gift of salvation, the Holy Spirit empowers him or her with at least one spiritual gift. From that point, it is that person's responsibility, with the aid of spiritual leadership, to identify and cultivate that gift. These gifts equip believers to serve mightily in the local church. Believers are encouraged in 1 Peter 4:10 to serve others in their gifting, as good stewards. Since God has entrusted us with spiritual gifts, we must use them to benefit others rather than to promote ourselves.

God has blessed each of us with a gift that is perfect for our ministry purposes. Our behavioral tendencies are connected to the gifting that the Holy Spirit has assigned to us. Operating in our assigned area is essential to our service to God. It helps us determine where to focus our time and effort for the greatest impact in God's kingdom. Church leaders are responsible to ensure that their members serve in God-ordained areas of ministry. Biblical instruction should be reserved for those who have the gift of teaching. Simply having the desire or willingness to teach should not be the qualifying factor. There is strong condemnation in James 3:1–2 of those who appoint themselves to teach God's Word to other believers. James informed his listeners about the responsibility and accountability of the teaching ministry. Teachers must be selective in their choice of words and in their delivery. During James's era, because of the

---

8 "What Are Common Attributes of Teachers?", *Institute in Basic Life Principles*, last visited April 29, 2020, https://iblp.org/questions/what-are-common-characteristics-teachers.

elevated status of teachers in the life of the church, it was not uncommon for people to desire to become teachers even though they were not fit to function in that capacity. Because of this, James did not want people to be drawn to teaching without a clear understanding of the tremendous responsibility that this ministry entails.

Churches should manage the teaching ministry with caution. Teachers should not be selected primarily according to ability. As with the other spiritual gifts, spiritual maturity, age, health, talents, skills, and character should also be considered when making assignments. Jesus offers a stern warning against unteachable and unrepentant teachers in Matthew 15:14 (NIV): "Leave them; they are blind guides. If the blind lead the blind, both will fall into a pit." Note that He addresses both the blind teachers and their blind followers. Both will ultimately meet their demise. Jesus rebuked one of His main adversaries, the Pharisees, who served as teachers. They were beyond hope, blinded by their own sense of self-righteousness. The Pharisees misunderstood God's Word, dwelling on external matters as the source of impurity rather than attributing uncleanness to their own sin. They failed to instruct people that sin was the source of contamination. As a result, their hearts as well as the hearts of their followers, turned to wickedness. Jesus executed judgement and wrath against both parties, "giving them over" (cf. Hos. 4:17).

We must be cautious lest we duplicate the same errors in our contemporary churches. Pastors and teachers must never attempt to water down the truth and resort to becoming crowd pleasers. When entertaining the congregation becomes the focus, doctrinal integrity is compromised, and sin diffuses rapidly. The apostle Paul charged the pastors at Ephesus in Acts 20:28 (NLT): "So guard yourselves and God's people. Feed and shepherd God's flock—his church, purchased with his own blood—over which the Holy Spirit has appointed you as leaders." Spiritual leaders are accountable to God for the teaching ministry of the local church body.

Today's churches should be guided by the scriptures when appointing individuals to serve as teachers or in any other ministry capacities. The local church should never become a spiritual free for all, a disorganized gathering where everyone clashes, and anyone is permitted to do anything at any time. We must be guided by Paul's call for order in 1 Corinthians 14:40 (NIV), "Let all things be done decently and in order." God established a culture whereby spiritual gifts can operate effectively. When spiritual gifts lean toward an unscriptural focus, including self-promotion, it grieves the Holy Spirit and discredits the work. Furthermore, in Romans 12:6–8, the apostle Paul stresses that our gifts vary, and we should use them appropriately to minister.

What happens when there is a vacancy in the teaching ministry, and no one is gifted to provide instruction? In this case, the church's leadership must exercise spiritual discretion. While they prayerfully seek a gifted teacher, the leadership may decide to pursue the following options: (1) temporarily assign double duties to established teachers or (2) train and develop others who demonstrate the potential to fill the vacant assignment temporarily. In executing the two options, church leadership must clearly communicate beforehand that these teacher placements are temporary solutions. No one should be led to believe otherwise. The culture of our local churches should be infused with love, peace, and harmony, in accordance with God's Word. There is no place for self-promotion, favoritism, boasting, or envy.

In summary, an effective teaching ministry is essential to the Church's growth and survival. We must refrain from adopting false presumptions about spiritual gifts. When believers deviate from God's established plan for ministry, the entire body suffers. As those who are gifted in teaching assume their rightful places, our local congregations will experience renewal, restoration, and revival.

Teaching in the New Testament

Biblical instruction was very impactful in the early church. The following examples give us a glimpse of the significance of the ministry of teaching during this era:

- Teaching is a charge (1 Tim. 4:10–11, NIV)

- Teaching with qualifications (2 Tim. 2:2, NIV)

- Teaching equips believers (2 Tim. 3:16–17, NLT)

- Teaching with integrity (Tit. 2:7–8, NLT)

- Growing as a teacher (Heb. 5:12, NLT)

- Teaching is a calling (Jas. 3:1–2, NIV)

- Teaching about Christ blesses others (2 Jn. 1:9, KJV)

The gift of teaching, designed for edifying the body of Christ, is referenced in the following scriptures:

- Romans 12:7 (NIV)

- 1 Corinthians 12:28 (NIV)

- Ephesians 4:11–16 (NIV)

We cannot omit the most profound instructor of all time, Jesus, the Master Teacher. The Lord is addressed as "teacher" numerous times in the gospels. The following references provide evidence of Jesus's teaching during this era:

- Jesus teaches in the synagogues (Matt. 4:23, KJV)

- Jesus's teaching amazes the crowd (Matt. 7:28, KJV)

- Jesus instructs his disciples privately (Mk. 4:34, KJV)

- Jesus teaches the crowd (Mk. 6:34, KJV)

- Jesus teaches in a boat (Lk. 5:3, KJV)

- Jesus's teaching supersedes all (Lk. 6:40, NIV)

- Jesus encounters Nicodemus (Jn. 3:1, KJV)

- Jesus credits His teaching to God (Jn. 7:16, KJV)

- Jesus's teaching acknowledged by Martha (Jn. 11:28, NIV)

- Jesus teaches on eternal life (Matt. 19:16, KJV

- Jesus's acknowledged as teacher by his enemies (Matt. 22:16, 24, KJV)

Jesus's teaching was informative, logical, supported by Old Testament evidence, well-illustrated, documented by divine power, original, and uniquely authoritative (Matt. 7:28). "When officers once were sent to arrest Him, they returned to their superiors empty-handed, exclaiming: 'No one ever spoke the way this man does,'" (Jn. 7:46, NIV).[9]

---

9 Wayne Jackson, "Jesus: The Master Teacher," *Christian Courier,* last visited April 29, 2020, https://www.christiancourier.com/articles/1497–jesus-the-master-teacher.

Motivational Tendencies

The seven motivational gifts of Romans 12 are practical in nature and describe the inner motivations of the Christian servant. These spiritual gifts produce certain motivating or influencing tendencies that drive how believers relate to others and to their surroundings. The Holy Spirit infuses every believer with qualities that shape their overall perspective on life. Because of this, those with the gift of teaching will find themselves unconsciously acting out specific inborn tendencies. This is an indication of our Creator's unique workmanship.

People gifted in teaching are passionate about validating biblical truth. These individuals enjoy investigating to gain knowledge and insight. They frequently spend extensive time studying the Word of God, uncovering information that others have either overlooked or dismissed. Teachers will question anything that seems inaccurate because they desire to maintain doctrinal integrity. This helps to keep the church focused on truth.

Have you been endowed with the gift of teaching? Do you become disturbed when false doctrine is presented? Do you challenge statements made by other teachers? Are you sometimes impractical, analytical, and unemotional?

As you continue in your quest to identify and confirm your gift(s), determine whether these motivational tendencies match your own. If they do, you are already reaping the joy that comes with such a beautiful ornament—the gift of teaching. If the attributes listed do not reflect your motivational tendencies, I encourage you to continue seeking the Lord in the validation of your spiritual gift(s).

Let us see what it is like to observe people and circumstances through the eyes of teaching. The following list provides common attributes shared by those with this spiritual gift.

- Those who operate in the gift of teaching search diligently for truth. They study untiringly while navigating through scripture, seeking answers that validate truth.

- Teachers guard the church against apostasy and help keep the body of Christ focused on truth. These gifted believers flinch when others present false doctrine. They do not honor experience over the authority of scripture.

- Those who operate in the gift of teaching may place a great deal of emphasis on original language—the original words used in scripture and their meanings.

- Teachers instinctively question any doctrine that seems faulty. This uneasiness usually motivates teachers to conduct research to seek answers that validate truth.

- Teachers delight in research. When they conduct research and reach a conclusion, they feel obligated to share their findings with others. Teachers may also attempt to explain how they arrived at this information. Teachers mistakenly assume that others will appreciate the research because they were fascinated by the process.

- Teachers find gratification in uncovering insights that others have either overlooked or considered insignificant. Also, teachers become excited about discovering and disseminating new information, such as stories, articles, and videos. Unfortunately, others may not share the same enthusiasm.

- Usually, believers with this motivational gift are not hesitant to challenge statements made or ideas presented by other teachers. This is an example of "iron sharpening iron" (cf. Prov. 27:17), which is a positive outcome of the teacher's passion for verifying information.

- Those who are gifted in teaching have excellent verbal communication skills; they articulate themselves well.

- Gifted teachers are well disciplined, as evidenced by their excellent study habits. They usually have great organizational skills.

- People who have the gift of teaching are very insightful. They can recognize patterns of behavior in situations, which allows them to expose problems unnoticed by others.

- Because of their passion for studying, teachers may have to force themselves to back away from their studies to maintain a balanced life.

- Sometimes teachers find it difficult to accept the views of others. Hence, it may be challenging for such individuals to receive biblical instruction from other teachers.

- Because teachers are exceptionally knowledgeable, they may become prideful, authoritative, or domineering. This causes them to feel superior to those who do not share their gift.

- Teachers experience ultimate joy and satisfaction when others learn and apply God's Word to their lives.

Finally, a teacher's motivation is to discover and validate biblical truth. Such believers are driven by a desire to present truth from a sound theological perspective.

3 C's—Characteristics, Challenges, and Choices

While each person in the body of Christ is unique, it is not unusual for those who operate in the same motivational gift to demonstrate common characteristics, to experience common challenges, and to serve in similar choices, or capacities in ministry.

Characteristics

While everyone in the body of Christ is unique, a believer who operates in the gift of teaching may possess several of the following characteristics.

- Accurate presenter of biblical truth

- Great communicator

- Enjoys study and investigation

- Uses biblical illustrations

- Detests scripture used out of context

- Strives to be objective rather than subjective

- Has an extensive vocabulary

- Starts with scripture when answering questions

- Is intellectual and analytical

- Exercises much discipline

- Has strong convictions based on solid research

- Believes God's truth is life-transforming

- Searches for an understanding behind ideas or concepts

- Is self-motivated

- Makes difficult concepts easy to understand

- Insightful

Although each person's behavior will vary according to factors such as age, gender, culture, environment, background, temperament, and experiences, it is common for those who have the motivational gift of teaching to demonstrate these characteristics.

Challenges

While everyone in the body of Christ is unique, a believer who operates in the gift of teaching may encounter some of the following challenges.

- Impractical and unemotional

- Reluctant to accept the views of others

- Sometimes labeled as unteachable

- Prideful because of knowledge

- Authoritative or domineering

- Easily distracted by love of new interests

- Argumentative

- Easily bored with routine

- Criticizes the overuse of practical applications

- Argues and debates over insignificant points

- Enthusiastically distributes truth or knowledge intended for other teachers and not a broader audience

It is important that we acknowledge these challenges and pray diligently to overcome each. As we minister, God's purpose for spiritual gifts must be at the forefront. He established a standard where spiritual gifts can operate in excellence. When we lean toward a carnal focus, Christ's ministry is compromised. This leads others to discredit the gifts and bypass the benefits they provide. As we stand on the pillar of Philippians 4:13, we can overcome all challenges through Christ, who gives us strength.

Choices (Areas of Service)

While this list is not comprehensive, it can be used as a guide for directing those who are passionate about identifying and operating in their area of spiritual giftedness. The chart below provides the following: 1) suggested positions or areas of service, 2) descriptions of the positions or areas of service, 3) abilities and best personality traits for each position, and 4) the type of ministry or the specific group for whom the person is passionate about serving.[10]

> "YOUR GIFT IS GOD'S GIFT TO YOU; WHAT YOU DO WITH IT IS YOUR GIFT TO GOD." ~ UNKNOWN

---

10 Gilbert and Spear, 2002.

Ministry Opportunities: Teaching

Position	Description	Characteristics	Passionate About:
Adult Bible Study Teacher	Responsible for instructing adults in a classroom setting	*Abilities*: Communicates well with others; able to speak in front of a group *Personality Traits:* Dependable, expressive, and compassionate.	Teaching and leading a group of people; discipling others
Financial Counselor	Responsible for instructing pupils in personal and church finances, using biblical principles	*Abilities:* Effective communicator, skillful in business and finances *Personality Traits:* Trustworthy, honest, discreet, empathetic, and dependable	Teaching and leading members to be good managers of their resources

Pre-school Sunday School Teacher	Expected to teach, reach, and minister to preschoolers with the help of other leaders within the class	*Abilities:* Able to communicate well with children *Personality Traits:* Dependable, expressive, compassionate, nurturing, and patient	Nurturing groups of children; teaching and leading children to Jesus

This chart serves as a guide to help teachers identify opportunities for serving. Here are other suggested positions or areas of service a gifted teacher may consider.

- Christian Education: Christian education director, children's director, youth director, Sunday school superintendent

- Speaking: church announcements, motivational speeches, readings, sermonettes

- Teaching: Bible study groups, discipleship groups, new members classes, small groups, Sunday school classes, training

Other influencing factors drive a person's ability to minister, including age, level of spiritual maturity, and overall health (physical and emotional). Collaborate with your local church leadership to develop your passions in ministry. Your spiritual advisors can assist you in selecting suitable options that are readily available within your local church.

Vision Enhancement

The motivational gifts function like a pair of eyeglasses, maximizing our spiritual vision. The gifts affect how we see life and respond to the needs around us. While prescriptive lenses correct or improve physical eyesight, these seven gifts alter or readjust spiritual sight. Like corrective lenses, as we "wear" these gifts, they serve as a remedy for impaired spiritual vision. They also influence our ability to focus on serving the body of Christ. To enhance physical vision, we must be willing to seek assistance in correcting our defective eyesight. The same is true of our spiritual vision. Consider physical nearsightedness and farsightedness. These are two common defects that can improve with proper intervention. Spiritual gifts can do the same thing for our spiritual vision.

- People who are spiritually nearsighted lack foresight and can only judge what is in front of them. Since such people are short-sighted, they cannot readily see distant images, which appear blurry. Visual accuracy is limited to only what is up close—the obvious.

- Spiritually farsighted individuals, on the other hand, can clearly see distant images, but objects that are in front of them appear blurry. Farsighted people can only judge images at a great distance.

Both visual impairments, nearsightedness and farsightedness, require prescriptive lenses for visual enhancement. It is amazing how these lenses help remedy both defects and improve overall vison. Likewise, if our spiritual eyesight is defective, we must be willing to receive the remedy that the Holy Spirit prescribes in the form of spiritual gifts.

Those who operate in the motivational gifts of the Spirit must clearly see people and circumstances through the lenses of their designated gifts. If we are to serve others in the body of Christ in an effective manner, our ability to focus on spiritual matters cannot be impaired. Believers who are spiritually nearsighted lack discretion in the things of God and cannot see the big picture. They are only capable of judging what is in front of them—the obvious. To nearsighted believers, any consideration outside of their apparent reach seems blurry. On the other hand, Christians who are spiritually farsighted tend to overlook what is directly in front of them.

In these instances, defective vision represents believers who misrepresent or abuse their spiritual gift(s), operating outside of their divine scope. Here is good news: both visual defects can be remedied. Almighty God, the Ultimate Designer, has provided corrective spiritual lenses that supersede those of any earthly optometrist.

Correcting Nearsightedness in Teaching

Persons gifted in teaching must be careful of becoming spiritually nearsighted, lacking foresight and only judging what is right in front of them. Here, nearsightedness symbolizes teachers promoting their personal agenda or leaning toward their personal weaknesses, i.e., the challenges detailed in the previous section. They should never become short-sighted, offering an explosive lesson sprinkled or masked with sarcasm. On the other hand, teachers should consistently communicate biblical truth. To achieve this, they must extend their spiritual vision into the distance. This takes place as teachers demonstrate humility and compassion toward their listeners.

Teachers are to be good stewards of every word that they utter. They are accountable to God for guiding or misguiding their listeners. Listening is an active process that involves understanding, assessing, and responding to what is heard. When a sarcastic teacher demonstrates carnality, the listener's ability to achieve these three components is compromised. Conversely, listeners may not receive the maximum spiritual benefit otherwise intended. Ephesians 4:15 serves as a reminder that we are to "speak the truth in love" as we endeavor to grow to become more like Christ. People will readily learn and apply God's truth as the Word is presented from a pure heart, evidenced by constructive speech. We must correct defective vision, spiritual nearsightedness, and strive to envision more distant images.

Correcting Farsightedness in Teaching

Believers gifted in teaching must also be careful of becoming spiritually farsighted. Focusing primarily on distant images or the big picture may cause one to miss the obvious—what is directly in front of us. Here, farsightedness represents every teacher's distant goal—to receive accolades for his or her conclusive research; consequently, their desire to impress their superiors with their research skills may override their true focus. Their focus shifts from the students' needs to their own. Teachers may be driven to see only distant images of personal achievement without considering what is right in front of them—the needs of their students.

Nearsightedness symbolizes a teacher's ability to discern those needs. Instead of focusing on the distant image, teachers must shift their focus to accommodate their listeners. They must never become so intense or farsighted that they miss the Holy Spirit's instructions for communicating biblical relevancy. Teachers should not persist in sharing insignificant off-topic information. While conducting research is therapeutic for teachers, students may perceive the unrelated knowledge as dull or boring. This impaired vision (farsightedness) can be corrected. Teachers must focus instead on the close and obvious—presenting relevant material that spiritually benefits their target audience. There is no room in the body of Christ for self-promotion. As we minister to others, it is vital to present information as the Holy Spirit leads. Teachers must remedy this spiritual farsightedness and strive to envision close-up images as well.

Vision Maintenance

Maintaining optimum spiritual vision is crucial. Once we are suitably matched to our Designer's eyewear, we must strive to keep them looking like new. Our spiritual lenses should remain free of spots and smears that can affect our focus. Spots and smears may symbolize the marring effects of our gifts if we become distracted. For example, distractions in the form of gifts that you don't possess but are attempting to operate in are like a spot or a smear. We must do whatever it takes to remove these smudges by reattaching to our God-infused spiritual gift, thereby enhancing our spiritual focus.

We must be intentional when it comes to maintaining and enhancing our visual health. The Ultimate Designer, through His Son, Jesus, set the example of how to boost spiritual vision. He engaged in spiritual disciplines such as study, meditation, prayer (solitude and silence), fasting, worship, service, and fellowship with other believers. Likewise, our spiritual vision will be enhanced as we practice the following.

- Study—Read and study God's Word for guidance and direction.

- Meditate—Ponder God's Word to maintain spiritual focus.

- Pray—Commune with God (solitude) and listen to Him (silence).

- Fast—Abstain from food or other distractors for a designated period.

- Worship—Engage in private and corporate worship, which connects us to God.

- Serve—Assist others compassionately, as Jesus did.

- Fellowship—Interact with other believers for encouragement and to equip each other for service.

As we engage in these maintenance practices, we will achieve the Designer's fashionable look. In addition, our vision will be remarkably enhanced, and our spiritual focus will be maximized. We will see objects at any distance, for we will have been fitted with the Ultimate Designer's eyewear. While optometrists utilize digital measurements to ensure an accurate and precise prescription, the Ultimate Designer operates with a precision that is unmatchable.

Finally, the gift of teaching is a unique adornment assigned by the Holy Spirit. Once believers receive confirmation of this gift, they will seek to achieve clearer vision through the lens of the cross. Jesus, the Anointed One, will be their focal point and example, as they exercise this spiritual gift in love and faithfulness.

As they fully trust God, the Ultimate Designer, and "wear" the lenses correctly, they will serve the body of Christ joyfully and effectively. The Holy Spirit has assigned the eyewear of teaching to enhance spiritual vision by adding or subtracting focusing power to the lives of believers. I have shared several guarantees that accompany this corrective remedy. The spiritual lenses of teaching prescribed by the Holy Spirit are:

- Progressive—they enable wearers to see both near and far

- Shatterproof—they are reliable and unbreakable

- Impact-resistant—they withstand any opposing or colliding force

- Scratch-resistant—they cannot be scratched or damaged

In addition, the frames attached to these spiritual lenses have the following features:

- Spring-loaded—they are less likely to be bent or warped

- Silicone Nose Pads—they prevent the eyeglasses from slipping

- Straps—they hold the glasses firmly in place

Congratulations! You have experienced spiritual eyesight through the lenses of teaching. Your knowledge and appreciation of this gift have been expanded. Since it is imperative that you identify, cultivate, and operate in your assigned gifts (1 Pet. 4:10; 1 Cor. 12 and 14), I encourage you to prayerfully confirm and validate your divine endowment. Discovering and confirming your spiritual gifts will help you remain in your ministry lane, thereby avoiding a head-on collision.

Have you been called to present sound biblical instruction to the body of Christ? If so, praise the Lord for adorning you with such a precious ornament—the gift of teaching. I encourage you to continue to seek the Lord in the cultivation and operation of your divine gift. If you need further guidance in identifying your gift, prayerfully navigate through the following chapters and continue to review the remaining motivational gifts of the Spirit for identification and confirmation.

The Gifted Believer's Prayer:

Father, I come to You in the name of Jesus concerning my spiritual gift. Please remove my desire to sin and forgive me for all my shortcomings. Thank you for empowering me with the precious gift of teaching. My desire is to be a worthy steward of the gifting that the Holy Spirit has assigned to me. Help me to overcome the challenges associated with the spiritual gift of teaching. Lead me in dedicated service as I study diligently and provide biblical instruction to those who desire to hear from you. May Your Word transform and impact people for Christ's kingdom. Amen.

CHAPTER 4
THROUGH THE LENSES OF ENCOURAGEMENT

> "IF IT IS TO ENCOURAGE,
> THEN GIVE ENCOURAGEMENT."
> ~ ROMANS 12:8 (NIV)

Just as prescriptive lenses improve physical vision, the motivational spiritual gifts of Romans 12 enhance our spiritual vision. Each gift functions like a pair of lenses, sharpening our spiritual focus as we serve others in the body of Christ. These gifts are frequently cited as "motivational gifts" because they are practical in nature and describe the inner motivations of gifted believers. Each believer has inherent motivational tendencies that drive the way he or she responds to various circumstances. The spiritual gifts affect how we see life and respond to the needs around us. As the Ultimate Designer, the Holy Spirit infuses each of us with a customized spiritual gift, which allows us to see people and circumstances through a specific set of lenses that remedy our impaired vision.

The Designer's Eyewear promotes godly and righteous living as a prerequisite for operating in the seven areas of spiritual giftedness. In the prelude to Romans 12, the apostle Paul urged the church in Rome to present their bodies as living sacrifices (12:1–2). He went on to urge them to offer humble service in the body of Christ (12:3). In addition, regenerated believers will also possess the fruit of the Spirit of Galatians 5:22–23—love, joy, peace, longsuffering, gentleness, goodness, faith, meekness, and temperance. Accordingly, as Spirit-filled believers wear the Designer's prescriptive lenses or spiritual eyewear, their vision will align more closely with how God views the world.

This book is based on the presumption that love conquers all. Immediately following the list of spiritual gifts, the apostle Paul further challenged the church to translate love into action (Rom. 12:9–21). He emphasized the sincerity, devotion, zeal, fervor, joy, compassion, and empathy demonstrated through genuine love. True disciples of Christ will exhibit love when operating in their spiritual giftedness. The supremacy of love always overrules the desire to disrupt the flow of the church's mission. We should never allow spiritual giftings to supersede Christian character. On the contrary, character should rise to the forefront while the gifting lags slightly. It is futile to attempt to exercise a spiritual gift without blending it with genuine affection and consideration of others. The apostle Paul eloquently expresses this spiritual truth in 1 Corinthians 13:1 (NIV): "If I speak in the tongues of men and angels, but do not have love, I am only a resounding gong or a clanging cymbal." *The Designer's Eyewear* is written with the notion that each spiritual gift is implemented and aligned with God's Word.

Gift Overview

The Ultimate Designer, God Almighty, is dedicated to presenting various options and exclusives in designer eyewear just for you. In this chapter, I present one of the seven options, the fourth motivational spiritual gift of Romans 12, the gift of encouragement (exhortation). The gift of encouragement and the gift of exhortation are synonymous. The NIV uses the term "encouragement," and the KJV uses "exhortation." As with the other spiritual gifts, the Holy Spirit assigns this gift to certain believers. It is a supernatural endowment where one draws near to others in times of need, strengthening and encouraging them with God's Word, persuading them to take courage in the face of adversity and empowering them to become spiritually mature in Christ, giving them hope by offering a biblical perspective. Persons gifted in encouragement may steer other believers toward spiritual growth and development by counseling, teaching, mentoring, and discipling them.

Amid a world plagued with disappointments, discouragement, and disdain, there is a need for godly encouragement. A remarkable transformation takes place when downtrodden individuals are inspired and motivated by gifted encouragers. Those with the gift of encouragement are passionate about boosting other people's morale. Encouragers are quite versatile in that they can lift and stimulate others as well as challenge and rebuke them. Encouragers find pleasure in using their time and talents to foster spiritual growth and maturity in others.

Many false perceptions are associated with the gift of encouragement. These are based on biased thinking and lack of understanding. Some mistakenly believe that any spiritual leader who is cheerful and enthusiastic operates in the gift of encouragement. Another popular misconception is that leaders who possess this gift should motivate and inspire their followers but never reprimand.

Every spiritual leader who has a cheerful and enthusiastic demeanor is not necessarily gifted in encouragement. This is an inaccurate way of regarding this motivational spiritual gift. While many believers, as well as non-believers, are cheerful and enthusiastic by nature, not all of them possess this gift. A spiritual gift is a supernatural endowment bestowed upon a believer by the Holy Spirit. God's criteria for this selection is beyond human comprehension. As the Spirit infuses a person with the gift of encouragement, that individual becomes empowered to serve explosively. The motivational spiritual gifts may be expressed through certain personality traits, but these alone do not serve as primary indicators of the gifts.

The gift of encouragement was not designed to suit any specific personality trait. Many church leaders are cheerful and enthusiastic, but that does not qualify them to minister as gifted encouragers. They may sport radiant smiles and appear to be jolly or lively, but they still may lack the basic attributes of an encourager. More important than an appearance of liveliness is a person's ability to passionately steer others into reaching their potential in Christ. Some encouragers are optimistic, motivating, and inspiring but do not have upbeat personalities. This is not a shortcoming. Again, personality and character traits cannot serve as primary indicators of spiritual gifts. The impact of the gift of encouragement transcends all behavioral characteristics. It involves more than being cheerful and enthusiastic, upbeat, or positive. The gift of encouragement is a divine calling that points others to God's sovereignty and unconditional love.

Another misconception is that people gifted in encouragement should motivate and inspire but never reprimand. This is untrue. An encourager's aim is to propel other believers into spiritual growth and maturity. As an encourager ministers to others under the Holy Spirit's guidance, he or she must speak the truth in love. When the pressures of life bombard an individual, hope must be offered from a biblical perspective. At times, this may involve communicating a rebuke or sharp disapproval of a specific behavior. According to Hebrews 4:12 (NIV), the "word of God is alive and active. Sharper than any double-edged sword, it penetrates even to dividing soul and spirit, joints and marrow; it judges the thoughts and attitudes of the heart." In this passage, God's Word "penetrating" signifies that it reaches a person's heart. The heart of a person, which is the center of all human activity, houses a person's motives and feelings (cf. Prov. 4:23, ESV).

As we are steered toward spiritual maturity, our hearts will be impacted by God's Word. "The Word of God acts as a sharp sword that inflicts deadly wounds. The sinner 'dies' or becomes dead to their former hopes."[11] It is a good thing that God's Word exposes our inner thoughts, intentions, and motives. God's truth exposes sinners, hypocrites, and self-deceivers. It also exposes secret sins, destructive emotions, and contaminating tendencies. Any one of these may hinder a believer's spiritual advancement. Encouragers serve God as they boldly communicate truth. That truth, inspired by the Holy Spirit, may be motivating or even challenging at times. If listeners embrace it, the end results will reflect spiritual growth and maturity.

---

11 *Jamieson-Fausset-Brown Bible Commentary*

Encouragement in the New Testament

The following scripture references provide a glimpse of the ministry of encouragement during the New Testament era.

- Timothy encourages with sound doctrine (Tit. 1:9, NIV)

- Timothy is charged to encourage (2 Tim. 4:2, NIV)

- Barnabas is the "Son of Encouragement" (Acts 4:36, NIV)

- Barnabas encourages the church family (Acts 11:23–24, NIV)

- Judas and Silas encourage the church (Acts 15:32, NIV)

The greatest encourager in the early church was the apostle Paul. The presence of God's Spirit in him stirred his passion to strengthen and console others. This led to Paul's quest to see God's people excel in spiritual maturity. His encouraging words carried an array of light to his congregants as well as to his fellow laborers in the gospel. The following scripture passages give us a glimpse of his role as an encourager.

- Paul encourages the shipwrecked passengers and crew (Acts 27:21–38, NIV)

- Paul and Barnabas encourage others (Acts 14:21–22, NIV)

- Paul encourages the churches he established (Acts 20:1–2, NIV)

- Paul speaks of his acts of encouragement (1 Thess. 2:11–12, NIV)

Paul's demonstration of encouragement is especially impacting in Acts 20. Paul was a prisoner on a ship traveling to Rome. After two weeks of being caught in a storm, the outlook was bleak. The passengers were sick, starving, and losing hope, fearing they were destined to die and become shipwrecked. In verse 22, Paul offers refreshing words of hope that there will be no loss of life—only destruction of the ship. He reassures the fearful passengers that his words will surely come to pass. This assurance was based on God's promise to His servant. Paul's unshakable faith and his unequivocal courage are demonstrated here. As the passengers and crew yielded to Paul's leadership, they were all encouraged. Indeed, Paul was not reluctant in offering strong words that ushered in strength and consolation. He did not hold back. What a dynamic encourager!

Likewise, we are often faced with difficult circumstances that appear to be hopeless. Our futile attempts to combat these issues with carnal ammunition leads to discouragement. This is a crafty tool that Satan uses to discredit our witness. In addition, discouragement blinds, deafens, and cripples believers on all levels. During the storms of life, we can all benefit from the ministry of encouragement. The Holy Spirit assigns this explosive gift to diffuse doubt, stimulate hope, and heighten trust in our sovereign God.

Motivational Tendencies

The seven motivational gifts of Romans 12 are practical in nature and describe the inner motivations of Christian servants. These spiritual gifts produce certain motivating or influencing tendencies that drive how we relate to others and to our surroundings. The Holy Spirit infuses us with qualities that shape our overall perspective on life. Because of this, we unconsciously act out specific inborn tendencies. This is an indication of our Creator's unique craftsmanship.

People gifted in encouragement are motivated to strengthen and console others amidst hopelessness. They view adversity as simply another opportunity to reveal God's glory and sovereignty. Such optimistic believers approach difficulties head on, encouraging others to be "steadfast and unmovable, always abounding in the work of the Lord" (1 Cor. 15:58, KJV). Encouragers motivate and inspire others to identify their purposes in the body of Christ. They are delighted when they can help others latch on to their spiritual gifts, talents, and special abilities.

Have you been endowed with the gift of encouragement? Do you frequently offer godly counsel to people in distress? Are you passionate about providing step-by-step instructions to those who seek your guidance? Do people seeking godly advice readily gravitate toward you? Perhaps you view trials and tribulations as golden opportunities for spiritual growth. Do you find yourself offering hope to other believers from a biblical perspective?

As you continue in your quest to identify and confirm your gift(s), determine whether these motivational tendencies match your own. If they do, then you are already reaping the joy that comes with such a beautiful ornament—the gift of encouragement. If the attributes listed do not reflect your motivational tendencies, I invite you to continue seeking the Lord in the validation of your spiritual gift.

Let's observe what it is like to view people and circumstances through the lenses of encouragement. The following list provides descriptions common to those who are endowed with this gift.

- Those with this gift are champions of encouragement. They are passionate about motivating others to reach their potential in Christ. When others fail to recognize their unique attributes, their sharp sense of discernment kicks in. Encouragers inspire others to stimulate their spiritual gifts, talents, and special abilities. They unselfishly hold other people's hands while steering them toward spiritual growth.

- Encouragers study, memorize, and meditate on God's Word. They desire to extract wisdom from the ocean of truth stored in their spirit. They also rely heavily upon scripture to validate their message.

- Encouragers prefer to apply scripture rather than investigate it. Unlike teachers, they do not have a passion for validating truth through investigation or research.

- Encouragers share a mutual attraction with their listeners. While encouragers are inherently drawn to people who seek motivation, those seeking help are also magnetized to them.

- Encouragers want so badly for scripture to provide a successful course of action to eliminate a problem that they may quote scripture out of context or imply that it says something that it does not, rationalizing that the ends justifies the means. This is a devastating trap for encouragers.[12]

- Encouragers call forth the best in others through encouragement and motivation. Thus, believers with the

---

12 "What are the seven motivational gifts?", *Institute in Basic Life Principles,* last visited April 29, 2020, https://iblp.org/questions/what-are-seven-motivational-gifts.

gift of encouragement can be great conversationalists, have excellent interpersonal skills, and tend to have outgoing personalities.

- Encouragers place utmost value on God's sovereignty. They believe that God is the ultimate source of all power and authority. As they minister to those who are experiencing adversity, encouragers always point them to God's omnipotence. As encouragers minister, they guide their listeners into developing an operative faith.

- Encouragers are usually active listeners, fully engaged and concentrating to fully comprehend and respond accordingly. As they listen intensively for details, they unconsciously connect others to biblical truth. The Holy Spirit serves as a pilot, guiding encouragers as they connect the dots and communicate spiritual truthfulness.

- Encouragers can occasionally become overzealous when giving advice, even though they are excellent counselors. Sometimes they are so intent on telling others how to view their situation from God's perspective that they fail to listen to the other person's perspective.

- To encouragers, trials are merely an opportunity for personal growth. "Though they are sympathetic to the needs of others, they see their pain through the lenses of God's sovereignty rather than through the lenses of suffering."[13]

- Encouragers may lead others through counseling, teaching, mentoring, or discipling. During these exchanges, they

---

13 Ibid.

prescribe step-by-step instructions or actions when responding to problems. Their passion to stimulate spiritual growth does not end with one session. Instead, encouragers follow up to ensure that hopelessness is displaced by an unwavering faith in Christ.

- Encouragers prefer offering spiritual assistance rather than physical assistance. Unlike those with the gift of service, they do not have a passion for meeting a need through hands-on assistance.

- People gifted in encouragement act as enablers, willing to help propel others to a higher level. They tirelessly sacrifice their time and talents to help transformation take place.

- People gifted in encouragement may be viewed as insensitive. Many times, in their zeal to help others move past their painful circumstances, they may fail to demonstrate empathy. Because encouragers see adversity as an opportunity for growth, they may disregard others' feelings. As they minister, they concentrate on changing the focus from fear to faith; therefore, they discourage any semblance of self-pity.

- Encouragers frequently interrupt others in conversation. Many times, in their zeal to respond to painful circumstances, they may fail to demonstrate common courtesy.

- Encouragers desire to see people improve and succeed. They have an ability to bring new life to people who have lost their determination and feel exhausted.

- Encouragers may find it difficult to turn off their "counseling valve," thereby offering unsolicited advice. Sometimes people desire to vent to others without receiving a rush of recommendations or suggestions.

- Encouragers tend to embrace all details, whether good or bad, as part of God's divine solution. They strongly advocate that all experiences work together to accomplish good for those who are called by God (Rom. 8:28, KJV). This highlights God's sovereignty and His ability to empower every aspect of our lives.

In conclusion, an encourager's motivation is to encourage and counsel. Encouragers are driven by a desire to steer others away from hopelessness, thereby helping them to achieve spiritual maturity.

3 *C*'s—Characteristics, Challenges, and Choices

While each person in the body of Christ is unique, it is not unusual for those who operate in the same motivational gift to demonstrate common characteristics, to experience common challenges, and to serve in similar choices, or capacities in ministry.

Characteristics

While everyone in the body of Christ is unique, a believer who operates in the gift of encouragement may possess several of the following characteristics.

- Optimistic, motivational, and inspiring

- Verbally encouraging and conversational

- Loves to engage in personal counseling

- Prefers applying scriptures rather than investigating them

- Prescribes practical advice

- Has a positive and uplifting attitude; desires to hear positive responses

- Is an active listener

- Demonstrates patience

- Works cooperatively with others

- Is a natural networker—gifted to make connections with people in key positions

- Is well-respected among his or her peers

- Excels in communication

- Perceives trials as opportunities for personal growth

- Prefers to solve problems quickly

- Is considerate of others' feelings

Although each person's behavior will vary according to factors such as age, gender, culture, environment, background, temperament, and experiences, it is common for those who have the motivational gift of encouragement to demonstrate these characteristics.

Challenges

While everyone in the body of Christ is unique, a believer who operates in the gift of encouragement may encounter some of the following challenges.

- Is outspoken and opinionated

- Is overtalkative and overzealous when sharing

- Tends to offer unsolicited advice

- Interrupts others frequently

- Is slightly overconfident

- Tends to be overly concerned

- Treats people as projects

- Underestimates the severity of personal obstacles

- Tends to use scripture out of context

- Gives up on those who appear to be uncooperative

We must acknowledge our challenges and pray diligently to overcome each. As we minister, God's purpose for spiritual gifts must remain at the forefront. He established a standard where spiritual gifts can operate in excellence. When we lean toward a carnal focus, Christ's ministry is compromised, which may lead others to discredit the gifts and bypass the benefits they provide. As we stand on the pillar of Philippians 4:13, we can overcome all challenges through Christ, who gives us strength.

Choices (Areas of Service):

While this list is not comprehensive, it can be used as a guide for directing those who are passionate about identifying and operating in their area of spiritual giftedness. The chart below provides the following: 1) suggested positions or areas of service, 2) descriptions of the positions or areas of service, 3) abilities and best personality traits for each position, and 4) the type of ministry or the specific group for whom the person is passionate.[14]

> "YOUR GIFT IS GOD'S GIFT TO YOU; WHAT YOU DO WITH IT IS YOUR GIFT TO GOD." ~ UNKNOWN

---

14 Gilbert and Spear, 2002.

Ministry Opportunities: Encouragement

Position	Description	Characteristics	Passionate About:
Christian Counselor	Offers a counseling approach using faith-based principles and psychological instruction to help people better manage and/or resolve life challenges	*Abilities:* Able to adhere to biblical beliefs but also follow ethical legal rules; must be licensed *Personality Traits:* Empathetic, compassionate, patient, and trustworthy	Helping others regain hope for their lives, which is found in Jesus Christ
Single Activities Coordinator	Responsible for planning and organizing regular activities for single adults for the purpose of fun, fellowship, and spiritual edification	*Abilities:* Good physical health, planning and organizational skills *Personality Traits:* Dependable leader	Planning activities for fun, fellowship, and spiritual edification

Support Group Director	Coordinates and oversees the support group ministry, which involves determining the need for specific target groups	*Abilities:* Good organizational skills *Personality Traits:* Compassionate and dependable	Reaching and nurturing people at their point of need

This chart serves as a guide in helping the gifted encourager identify opportunities. Here are other recommendations for serving in this gift.

- Counseling: financial, pastoral, and group

- Shepherding: discipling, leading any target group, mentoring, pastoring, overseeing of staff

- Staffing: interviewing, placement and recruiting, training

- Teaching: Bible study groups, discipleship groups, small groups, training

Other influencing factors drive a person's ability to minister, including age, level of spiritual maturity, and overall health (physical and emotional). I recommend that you collaborate with your local church leadership to develop your passions in ministry. Your spiritual advisors can assist you in selecting suitable options that are readily available within your local church.

In summary, believers gifted in encouragement are motivated by a desire to strengthen and console others during times of hopelessness or despair. They view adversity as a golden opportunity to reveal God's glory and sovereignty.

Vision Enhancement

The motivational gifts function like a pair of eyeglasses, maximizing our spiritual vision. The gifts affect how we see life and respond to the needs around us. While prescriptive lenses correct or improve physical eyesight, these seven gifts alter or readjust spiritual sight. Like corrective lenses, as we "wear" these gifts, they serve as a remedy for impaired spiritual vision. They also influence our ability to focus on serving the body of Christ. To enhance physical vision, we must be willing to seek assistance in correcting our defective eyesight. The same is true of our spiritual vision. Consider physical nearsightedness and farsightedness. These are two common defects that can improve with proper intervention. Spiritual gifts can do the same thing for our spiritual vision.

- People who are spiritually nearsighted lack foresight and can only judge what is in front of them. Since such people are short-sighted, they cannot readily see distant images, which appear blurry. Visual accuracy is limited to only what is up close—the obvious.

- Spiritually farsighted individuals, on the other hand, can clearly see distant images, but objects that are in front of them appear blurry. Farsighted people can only judge images at a great distance.

Both visual impairments, nearsightedness and farsightedness, require prescriptive lenses for visual enhancement. It is amazing how these lenses help remedy both defects and improve overall vison. Likewise, if our spiritual eyesight is defective, we must be willing to receive the remedy that the Holy Spirit prescribes in the form of spiritual gifts.

Those who operate in the motivational gifts of the Spirit must clearly see people and circumstances through the lenses of their designated gifts. If we are to serve others in the body of Christ in an effective manner, our ability to focus on spiritual matters cannot be impaired. Believers who are spiritually nearsighted lack discretion in the things of God and cannot see the big picture. They are only capable of judging what is in front of them—the obvious. To nearsighted believers, any consideration outside of their apparent reach seems blurry. On the other hand, Christians who are spiritually farsighted often overlook what is directly in front of them.

In these instances, defective vision represents believers who misrepresent or abuse their spiritual gift(s), operating outside of their divine scope. Here is good news: both visual defects can be remedied. Almighty God, the Ultimate Designer, has provided corrective spiritual lenses that supersede those of any earthly optometrist.

Correcting Nearsightedness in Encouragement

Persons gifted in encouragement must be careful of becoming spiritually nearsighted, lacking foresight, and only judging what is in front of them. Here, nearsightedness symbolizes encouragers promoting their personal agenda or leaning toward their personal weaknesses, i.e., the challenges detailed in the previous section. Encouragers must not become short-sighted, focusing only on self. Instead, they must extend their spiritual vision into the distance by modeling the heart of Christ.

Encouragers must seek to overcome all obstacles that hinder their ability to operate successfully in this gift. While they are driven by a passion to evict hopelessness, encouragers may encounter certain challenges. If they fail to demonstrate proper listening etiquette and respect, their ministry of encouragement can be compromised. For instance, if they are frequently perceived as loquacious or overtalkative, their effectiveness as reputable counselors or advisors may be at stake. This is a clear indication of nearsightedness. In such instances, encouragers are fueled by their weakness—excessive talking. They are focusing on the obvious, fulfilling their desire to be heard. This short-sighted view inhibits encouragers from viewing more distant objects. Such objects include listening actively and responding to the needs of distressed individuals.

An encourager's ability to view these distant images can become blurred. When this visual defect occurs, encouragers can be labeled as "chatty" or "gabby." As a result, a person who would have otherwise benefited from godly counsel may dismiss both the message and the messenger. If encouragers hope to revitalize those who have lost their determination, they must focus on becoming active listeners. This requires encouragers to concentrate, comprehend, respond to, and remember what is being said.

Self-discipline is essential to operating in our spiritual gifts. Again, we must acknowledge these challenges and pray diligently to overcome them. As we minister, God's purpose for spiritual gifts must always be in the forefront. He establishes a standard whereby spiritual gifts can operate in excellence. When we lean toward a carnal focus, Christ's ministry is compromised, which may lead others to discredit the gifts and bypass the benefits that they provide. As we stand on the pillar of Philippians 4:13, we can overcome all challenges through Christ, who gives us strength.

Correcting Farsightedness in Encouragement

A gifted encourager must also be careful of becoming spiritually farsighted. Focusing primarily on distant images or the big picture may cause them to miss the obvious—what is directly in front of them. Here, farsightedness represents an encourager's enthusiastic desire to encourage and motivate through counseling. Hence, encouragers may be driven to see only images in the distance—the outcome of the sessions—without considering what's right in front of them, the distressed person's feelings. Gross insensitivity is a catalyst for destruction. When those who counsel demonstrate a lack of empathy for others, the outcome is jeopardized. Because encouragers view adversity and challenges as opportunities for growth, they may disregard the feelings of those who do not share their view. They fail to understand that the person in distress does not yet grasp this concept. As they minister, inspire, and motivate, encouragers are concentrating on changing an individual's perspective from fear to faith. During this process, they may mistakenly interpret an individual's feelings as indicators of self-pity. Then an encourager may begin to discourage any semblance of self-absorbed unhappiness.

Instead of focusing only on distant images or the outcome of a counseling session, encouragers must focus on what is right in front of them—other people's feelings. They must demonstrate empathy and never become so insensitive or farsighted that they miss the opportunity to demonstrate compassion. Such farsightedness can be corrected as encouragers focus on the obvious—the other person's heartfelt perspective. Encouragers must remember that their gift is a divine calling that points others to God's sovereignty and unconditional love.

Finally, like all believers, encouragers must always exhibit Christ's love when exercising their spiritual gift. The Holy Spirit endows us with the ability to minister effectively to His Church with a heavenly graceful flavor—the spirit of love. The supremacy of love must always supersede supernatural gifting. It is unprofitable to exercise a spiritual gift without blending it with genuine affection for others. The apostle Paul eloquently expresses this spiritual truth in 1 Corinthians 13:1 (NIV), "If I speak in the tongues of men and angels, but do not have love, I am only a resounding gong or a clanging cymbal."

Vision Maintenance

Maintaining optimum spiritual vision is crucial. Once we are suitably matched to our Designer's eyewear, we must strive to keep them looking like new. Our spiritual lenses should remain free of spots and smears that can affect our focus. Spots and smears may symbolize the marring effects of our gifts if we become distracted. For example, distractions in the form of gifts that you don't possess but are attempting to operate in are like a spot or a smear. We must do whatever it takes to remove these smudges by reattaching to our God-infused spiritual gift, thereby enhancing our spiritual focus.

We must be intentional when it comes to maintaining and enhancing our visual health. The Ultimate Designer, through His Son, Jesus, set the example of how to boost spiritual vision. He engaged in spiritual disciplines such as study, meditation, prayer (solitude and silence), fasting, worship, service, and fellowship with other believers. Likewise, our spiritual vision will be enhanced as we practice the following.

- Study—Read and study God's Word for guidance and direction.

- Meditate—Ponder God's Word to maintain spiritual focus.

- Pray—Commune with God (solitude) and listen to Him (silence).

- Fast—Abstain from food or other distractors for a designated period.

- Worship—Engage in private and corporate worship, which connects us to God.

- Serve—Assist others compassionately, as Jesus did.

- Fellowship—Interact with other believers for encouragement and to equip each other for service.

As we engage in these maintenance practices, we will achieve the Designer's fashionable look. In addition, our vision will be remarkably enhanced, and our spiritual focus will be maximized. We will see objects at any distance, for we will have been fitted with the Ultimate Designer's eyewear. While optometrists utilize digital measurements to ensure an accurate and precise prescription, the Ultimate Designer operates with a precision that is unmatchable.

Finally, the gift of encouragement is a unique adornment assigned by the Holy Spirit. Once believers receive confirmation of this gift, they should seek to achieve clearer vision through the lens of the cross. Jesus, the Anointed One, is our focal point and example as we exercise this spiritual gift in love and faithfulness. As we fully trust God, the Ultimate Designer, and "wear" the lenses of encouragement, we will minister with a touch of grace. The Holy Spirit has assigned the eyewear of encouragement to enhance spiritual vision by adding or subtracting focusing power to our lives. I have shared several guarantees that accompany this corrective remedy. The spiritual lenses of encouragement prescribed by the Holy Spirit are:

- Progressive—they enable us to see both near and far

- Shatterproof—they are reliable and unbreakable

- Impact-resistant—they withstand any opposing or colliding force

- Scratch-resistant—they cannot be scratched or damaged

In addition, the frames attached to these spiritual lenses have the following features:

- Spring-loaded—they are less likely to be bent or warped

- Silicone Nose Pads—they prevent the eyeglasses from slipping

- Straps—they hold the glasses firmly in place

Congratulations! You have experienced spiritual eyesight through the lenses of encouragement. Your knowledge and appreciation of this gift have been expanded. Since it is imperative that you identify, cultivate, and operate in your assigned gifts (1 Pet. 4:10; 1 Cor. 12 and 14), I encourage you to prayerfully confirm and validate your divine endowment. Discovering and confirming your spiritual gifts will help you remain in your ministry lane, thereby avoiding a head-on collision.

Have you confirmed that the act of encouraging others is your ministry focus? Do the motivations of an encourager guide your decisions and actions? If so, praise the Lord for adorning you with such a precious ornament—the gift of encouragement. I recommend that you seek the Lord in the cultivation and operation of your divine gift. If you need further guidance in identifying your gift, prayerfully navigate through the following chapters, and continue to review the remaining motivational gifts of the Spirit for identification and confirmation.

The Gifted Believer's Prayer:

Father, I come to you in the name of Jesus concerning my spiritual gift. From the rising of the sun until the going down of the same, you are worthy to be praised. Today, I offer godly repentance for my sins. Almighty God, from the fruit of my lips, I offer thanksgiving to you, for I appreciate this precious gift of encouragement. I treasure your Word, for it is perfect and complete. As I yield myself to your service, encouraging others, I ask for an impartation of wisdom from heaven. Help me to overcome all the challenges associated with this gift. May all that I do in your name bring glory and honor to you. Amen.

CHAPTER 5

Through the Lenses of Giving

"If it is giving, then give generously."
~ Romans 12:8 (NIV)

Just as prescriptive lenses improve physical vision, the motivational spiritual gifts of Romans 12 enhance our spiritual vision. Each gift functions like a pair of lenses, sharpening our spiritual focus as we serve others in the body of Christ. These gifts are frequently cited as "motivational gifts" because they are practical in nature and describe the inner motivations of gifted believers. Each believer has inherent motivational tendencies that drive the way he or she responds to various circumstances. The spiritual gifts affect how we see life and respond to the needs around us. As the Ultimate Designer, the Holy Spirit infuses each of us with a customized spiritual gift, which allows us to see people and circumstances through a specific set of lenses that remedy our impaired vision.

The Designer's Eyewear promotes godly and righteous living as a prerequisite for operating in the seven areas of spiritual giftedness. In the prelude to Romans 12, the apostle Paul urged the church in Rome to present their bodies as living sacrifices (12:1–2). He went on to urge them to offer humble service in the body of Christ (12:3). In addition, regenerated believers will also possess the fruit of the Spirit of Galatians 5:22–23—love, joy, peace, longsuffering, gentleness, goodness, faith, meekness, and temperance. Accordingly, as Spirit-filled believers wear the Designer's prescriptive lenses or spiritual eyewear, their vision will align more closely with how God views the world.

This book is based on the presumption that love conquers all. Immediately following the list of spiritual gifts, the apostle Paul further challenged the church to translate love into action (Rom. 12:9–21). He emphasized the sincerity, devotion, zeal, fervor, joy, compassion, and empathy demonstrated through genuine love. True disciples of Christ will exhibit love when operating in their spiritual giftedness. The supremacy of love always overrules the desire to disrupt the flow of the church's mission. We should never allow spiritual giftings to supersede Christian character. On the contrary, character should rise to the forefront while the gifting lags slightly. It is futile to attempt to exercise a spiritual gift without blending it with genuine affection and consideration of others. The apostle Paul eloquently expresses this spiritual truth in 1 Corinthians 13:1 (NIV): "If I speak in the tongues of men and angels, but do not have love, I am only a resounding gong or a clanging cymbal." *The Designer's Eyewear* is written with the notion that each spiritual gift is implemented and aligned with God's Word.

Gift Overview

The Ultimate Designer, God Almighty, is dedicated to presenting various options and exclusives in designer eyewear just for you. In this chapter, I present one of the seven options, the fifth motivational spiritual gift of Romans 12, the gift of giving. As with the other spiritual gifts, the Holy Spirit assigns this gift to certain believers. It is a supernatural gift that enables recipients to give their financial resources with joy and eagerness, without any ulterior motives that would benefit them.

Spirit-infused givers are passionate about sharing their financial assets as a means of glorifying their Creator. Those with this gift go above and beyond the call of duty. Their giving reflects a readiness to contribute more than is expected or required. Such believers are driven by a sense of urgency to use their financial blessings to meet specific needs. For such individuals, the act of giving gets their pulse racing. With a generous heart, they are unconsciously drawn to contribute to individuals, special projects, capital campaigns, or fundraisers.

Givers are invigorated as they fulfill needs that are often overlooked by others. Their supernatural intuition, blended with their God-given discernment, is noteworthy. They are further energized as they glorify God through the releasing of their financial resources. Those who are endowed with this gift do not seek recognition, commendations, or accolades in return for their gifts and have no desire to see their name displayed in flashy neon lights. In most instances, they are content with remaining anonymous. Ultimately, a giver's greatest joy comes in knowing that his or her contributions have touched God's heart.

This precious adornment, the gift of giving, has frequently been misunderstood, even within the body of Christ. In a society plagued by inflated egos, many individuals boast of their impressive contributions to various ministries and lavish projects. Are these acts truly motivated by a genuine desire to glorify God? Let us observe the following misconceptions about the gift of giving.

- A Christian endowed with the gift of giving can choose to contribute personal time rather than personal contributions.

- Every Christian who tithes regularly is endowed with the gift of giving.

- A Christian endowed with the gift of giving is obligated to fulfill all random financial appeals.

- Every Christian who possesses wealth and riches is endowed with the gift of giving.

One popular misconception is that the gift of giving is characterized by the contribution of one's personal time, not merely by personal finances. While God delights in believers offering their personal time in ministry, this does not exempt us from offering our financial resources, nor does it override the significance of monetary contributions. Furthermore, this belief does not constitute the makeup of one infused with the gift of giving. More often, a person who endorses this claim considers it more advantageous to give of their time rather than their financial resources. They often view the two—time and financial resources—as equivalent, conveniently swapping one for the other based on their best interests. This double-dealing does not reflect the attributes of a spiritually gifted giver. Understanding the scope of this gift does not require an advanced degree in theology. Either a person is gifted in giving, or he or she is not. True givers are distinctive—they stand out from the crowd. Believers who are infused with this gift can easily be distinguished from the masses. They religiously seek opportunities to give financially, they disperse their material assets liberally and cheerfully, they give from their abundance as well as their lack, and they offer high-quality gifts that reflect their standard of excellence.

Givers need reassurance that their decisions are in God's will. This is true whether they have little or much to give. To achieve this, they first give themselves sacrificially to the Lord's work. Once this occurs, their financial gifts follow. Since all believers must practice giving, Paul explained how the Macedonians "first gave their own selves to the Lord, and unto us by the will of God" (2 Cor. 8:5, KJV). Consequently, while spiritually gifted givers offer their personal time to promote ministry, they never infer or declare that it overrides their ability to offer financial support.

One cannot claim to be a gifted giver and then consistently maintain that time offered in serving Christ is a suitable substitute for contributing financially. Such people are deceiving themselves. People who promote this misconception deny the transforming power of biblical giving. Such individuals do not have the proper attitude or motive concerning this precious gift. Believers should be true to God as it relates to their motives and intentions. When people resort to treachery to justify nonconformance, they must be willing to bear the consequences. Ananias and Sapphira, the married couple illustrated in Acts 5, were models of such a deceptive practice. These two members of the church in Jerusalem secretly withheld their financial obligations from the Lord, and both experienced sudden death after lying to the Holy Spirit. While this example may be viewed as extreme, it is quite relevant, for "there are no locked doors or hidden closets for the Holy Spirit."[15] The secrets of a person's heart are no secret to God. Honesty and integrity prevail. As opposed to hinging on "time" or some other escape, gifted givers are prompted to edify the body of Christ through financial contributions. Consequently, those who are not motivated to share their financial assets to satisfy crucial needs should not boast of possessing the gift of giving. Instead, they should seek God for guidance in identifying, cultivating, and serving in their true spiritual gift. The gift of giving is characterized by an eagerness to give one's finances with joy and delight.

Contrary to popular belief, a Christian who tithes regularly is not necessarily endowed with the gift of giving. This is another false perception based on a lack of understanding. Many believers view tithing as a biblical mandate that touches God's heart. The tithe is the first 10 percent of a believer's income that is given to the local church. As a disciple of Christ, givers are proponents of tithing and believe it is a requirement for all to follow (cf. Gen. 14:19–20, Lev. 27:30–34, Neh. 10:35–37, Mal. 3:8–11, Matt. 23:3, Heb. 7:1–2). Tithing is foundational to givers and, therefore, is not an option. Givers view this act as a heart-to-heart deed—from one heart to another. God's heart is moved to bless the giver with 90 percent; inversely, the giver's heart is moved to reciprocate and bless God with 10 percent. According to Matthew 6:21 (NIV), "where your treasure is, there your

---

15 J. D. Greear, "5 Things God Teaches Us in the Tragic Deaths of Ananias and Sapphira," *J.D. Greear Ministries,* last visited April 29, 2020, https://jdgreear.com/blog/5–things–god–teaches–us–in–the–tragic–deaths–of–ananias–sapphira.

heart will be also." Thus, from one heart to another, tithing is an exchange of mutual love and admiration. It should, however, be given with pure motives. We should never attempt to swindle God by offering tithes in exchange for a personal blessing. Again, tithing is motivated by pure love.

While it is viewed as an act of Christian obedience, tithing alone does not qualify believers to be recipients of this spiritual gift. A believer's willingness to share financial substance through consistent tithing is commendable; however, the gift of giving begins where tithing ends. Those with the gift of giving raise the bar. While tithing is a mandate for all believers, spiritually gifted givers unconsciously exceed this mark. In addition to blessing the local body with their tithes and offerings, believers endowed with this gift seek other opportunities to share their finances. They are passionate about maximizing their potential to give, seeking wise investments and motivating others to contribute as well.

Those with the gift of giving rejoice when they perceive that their giving is an answer to someone else's prayer. Givers have a Spirit-infused passion to serve God by giving above and beyond what is required of them. Again, they unconsciously contribute far beyond their tithes to further the work of the kingdom. Finally, spiritually endowed givers view tithing as a springboard for diving into a pool of bountiful giving opportunities.

Here is another inaccurate view about the gift of giving. Many feel that one who possesses the gift should never turn down an opportunity to contribute. A Christian endowed with the gift of giving is not obligated to fulfill all random financial appeals. This is a misconception. God, through the Holy Spirit, is the author and dispenser of all spiritual gifts. He meticulously infuses givers with a heart that longs to satisfy financial needs. Believers who walk in this supernatural gift are drawn by God to share their personal finances. They have a built-in passion to meet needs without the pressure of outside appeals. Because they are good at managing their finances, givers contribute conservatively. They are not motivated by emotional appeals but by the Lord's leading. Givers resist being pressured to contribute to fanfares, such as flashy fundraisers or displays of financial pageantry. Instead, they prefer to assist in the following ways: supporting needy individuals they have been made aware of; contributing to other benevolent requests; supporting the local church's ministries, fundraisers, and special campaigns; contributing to missions and outreach initiatives; and satisfying financial needs overlooked by others. Their giving has no limitations, and their blessings have no boundaries.

Givers use their gifts to seek ways to discourage dependency, slothfulness, and extravagance. They establish safeguards to avoid the perception that their contributions are corrupt. Spirit-infused givers are cognizant that some recipients of their support are undisciplined in money matters. They are aware that many believers have not mastered biblical financial principles. As a result, givers will not allow themselves to be pressured beyond their deep-rooted passions. They do not give blindly but instead give insightfully. A giver's strong sense of accountability to God outweighs his or her temptation to appease people. Givers highly esteem the act of giving as a means of honoring their Heavenly Father.

There is another popular misconception associated with the gift of giving. Many falsely believe that a Christian who possesses wealth and riches is endowed with the gift of giving. On the contrary, many believers who are blessed with an abundance of material assets are unwilling to share their reserves. In Matthew 19:23–30 (NIV), Jesus speaks on the topic of the rich and the kingdom of God. He says, "it is easier for a camel to go through the eye of a needle than for a rich man to enter the Kingdom of God." In some cities at the time, the narrow gate for those on foot, located near the larger gate where wagons, camels, and other beasts entered the city, was known as the "needle's eye." Like all comparisons, it states a general fact—wealth can hinder our growth toward holiness.[16]

Wealth and riches may encourage a false spirit of independence, much like the church of Laodicea: "I am rich, have become wealthy, and have need of nothing" (Revelation 3:17, NASB). Rich people may subconsciously credit their accumulation of wealth to their hard work, intellectual capacity, networking connections, and/or business savvy. They may boast of dual attributes—brains and brawn or intelligence and physical stamina. Like the church of Laodicea, wealthy people can succumb to an attitude of self-reliance. This attitude blinds and deafens them to the cries of those less fortunate.

Wealthy believers thoughtlessly justify their reluctance or refusal to assist others financially, and they often spew out countless reasons for doing so. Such individuals frequently declare, "I got mine, so go get yours." They are quick to judge those who are impoverished by pointing out such individuals' weaknesses and mistakes. This is a strategy pulled from the wealthy person's "subconscious playbook" to justify their unwillingness to give. If they can convince themselves that the requestor is undeserving of monetary assistance, this further justifies and solidifies the

---

16 Ellicott's Commentary for English Readers

wealthy person's position. Also, one "can easily be tempted to judge a person or ministry based on a single incident that appears to reflect poor stewardship or lack of accountability, rather than taking the steps necessary to get an accurate account of the situation."[17] How disgraceful that believers who are financially blessed are frequently the worst critics of those who are less fortunate.

Wealth and riches may serve as a stumbling block in a believer's spiritual growth. It is utterly impossible for people who set their hearts upon their riches to enter heaven. Christ used an expression, denoting a difficulty altogether unconquerable by the power of man. Nothing less than the almighty grace of God will enable a rich man to get over this difficulty. Rich people cannot be saved in their worldliness, but they can be saved *from* their worldliness as they embrace Christ and His commands. Consequently, financial status does not qualify one for this spiritual gift. Instead, it is the openness of the heart to obey the Lord in matters of giving.

Financial expectations are greater for wealthy individuals. More money-related temptations afflict such people, according to Matthew 19:23. Rich people who overlook the poor will have to account for their actions. We should never pass up an opportunity to bless God by blessing others. Throughout the Bible, we are mandated to care for those who are impoverished. Proverbs 28:27 (NLT) declares, "Whoever gives to the poor will lack nothing, but those who close their eyes to poverty will be cursed." It is incorrect, however, to assume that wealthy Christians should distribute their finances senselessly. As good stewards of

---

17 "What are the seven motivational gifts?", *Institute in Basic Life Principles,* last accessed April 29, 2020, https://iblp.org/questions/what-are-seven-motivational-gifts.

God's blessings, they have an obligation to wisely manage the resources with which they have been entrusted. Like all believers, they must practice being resourceful and thrifty, not wasting money that could otherwise be used for ministry purposes.

Possessing wealth and riches is not a prerequisite for serving in this gift. The fact that a believer has acquired wealth does not qualify him or her to be a Spirit-infused giver. Individuals who masquerade as Christians but who demonstrate no compassion or empathy for the needy may require a spiritual "heart transplant." Their hearts have been hardened while their hands remain tight-fisted. Such people must adhere to Ezekiel 36:26 (NLT): "And I will give you a new heart, and I will put a new spirit in you. I will take out your stony, stubborn heart and give you a tender, responsive heart." Spiritually gifted givers feel "personally invested in the ministry or the life of the person to which they have given. Being part of another person's success brings the giver joy."[18] Again, a spiritually gifted giver's motives are pure. Many rich people contribute toward specific causes for some ulterior motive, such as tax write-offs, recognition, or accolades and praise. Spiritually gifted givers are driven by a deep passion to exalt the Savior through their monetary contributions. A pat on the back does not motivate them; only the act of giving does.

It is possible for believers who are not wealthy to be endowed with the gift of giving. Spiritually gifted givers, regardless of their financial status, will contribute from their abundance as well as their lack. Such individuals are generous, charitable, resourceful, and conscientious. Their passion to give wholeheartedly is not dependent upon their net worth. As the Holy Spirit infuses

---

18 Charles F. Stanley, "The Gift of Giving," *In Touch Ministries,* November 10, 2014, https://www.intouch.org/read/the-gift-of-giving.

such people with this spiritual gift, He also equips them with the ability to minister effectively. Such believers can achieve maximum results in their service to the Lord through their giving. God is no respecter of persons; therefore, He does not demonstrate partiality in granting spiritual gifts. Giving, as with every other motivational gift, is not confined to ethnicity, race, culture, economics, age, gender, denomination, location, or social status. God, in His sovereignty, chooses whom He pleases to fulfill various earthly ministry assignments.

Spiritually gifted givers are true champions of Christian stewardship. Indeed, they have mastered the biblical principles of giving. Givers entertain no thoughts that contradict God as sole owner of the entire universe; therefore, they regard giving as a privilege and an opportunity to honor the Great Giver. They stand unwaveringly upon the pillar of Psalm 24:1 (NIV), which states, "The earth is the LORD'S, and the fulness thereof; the world, and they that dwell therein." This scripture is reflected in the giver's heartfelt giving. Givers believe they must give back to the One who owns it all. A giver's attitude in sharing his or her financial resources aligns with the latter part of 2 Corinthians 9:7, which says God loves a cheerful giver. Such giving is characterized by an overwhelming sense of spiritual fulfillment.

Giving in the New Testament

Giving in the early church was quite widespread. The following examples give us a glimpse of the act of giving during that era.

- Giving in secret (Matt. 6:3–4, ESV)

- Giving reflects the heart (Matt. 6:19–21, KJV)

- Giving with an impure heart (Matt. 23:23, ESV)

- Giving your all (Mk. 12:41–44, ESV)

- Giving to those in need (Lk. 3:11, ESV)

- Giving to others unconditionally (Lk. 6:30, NIV)

- Giving liberally of your substance (Lk. 6:38, NIV)

- Using wealth wisely (Lk. 16:11, ESV)

- Giving out of poverty (Lk. 21:1–4, ESV)

- Sharing possessions among fellow believers (Acts 4:32–35, ESV)

- Contributing to the needs of the saints (Rom. 12:13, ESV)

- Exceeding expectations through giving (2 Cor. 8:3–5, NIV)

- Sowing and reaping through giving (2 Cor. 9:6, ESV)

- Giving cheerfully (2 Cor. 9:7, ESV)

- Contributing to good works (2 Cor. 9:8, ESV)

- Ministering through giving (2 Cor. 9:12, ESV)

- Loving money is the root of all evil (1 Tim. 6:10–11)

- Warning against loving money (Heb. 13:5, ESV)

- Giving to meet tangible needs (Jas. 2:15–16, NIV)

- Demonstrating love through giving (1 Jn. 3:17, NLT)

The gift of giving, designed for edifying the body of Christ, was also utilized in the church in Rome (Rom. 12:8).

While this list is quite extensive, it doesn't fully capture the plethora of scriptures that pertain to giving. Other applicable Bible verses can be found throughout the Old and New Testaments; however, this index is sufficient for usage by believers with the gift of giving as well as those who do not have this gift. It serves as a refresher for believers who engage in giving and a guide for believers who lag in giving. God has sanctioned each member of the body of Christ to give of their financial resources and has endowed certain ones with the gift of giving.

The Creator has commissioned some believers to edify His earthly ministry by giving in a supernatural way. Those who operate in this Holy Spirit-infused capacity are frequently presented with unique opportunities to give.

> In Acts 4:34–5:10, there is a significant description of people who had unusual opportunities to give. In the early church, Christian landowners often sold their property and other possessions and gave the proceeds to the church to care for those in need. One of those men was Barnabas. He sold his land and laid the money at the apostles' feet (Acts 4:36–37); but Ananias and Sapphira, as discussed earlier, sold their land and schemed to give only part of the money to the Lord's work. They lied and tried to deceive the apostles (Acts 5:1–10). It is interesting to compare the attitudes and the rewards those individuals received. Barnabas eventually accompanied the apostle Paul in much of their ministry. God killed Ananias and Sapphira on the spot because of their treachery.[19]

19 Larry Gilbert, "Do You Have the Spiritual Gift of Giving?", *ChurchGrowth.org*, last visited April 29, 2020, https://www.churchgrowth.org/do-you-have-the-spiritual-gift-of-giving/.

Unlike this couple, the gifted giver's contributions are a measurement of the giver's faith in God. As James 2:14–17 (NIV) reads, "What good is it, my brothers and sisters, if someone claims to have faith but has no deeds? Can such faith save them? Suppose a brother or a sister is without clothes and daily food. If one of you says to them, "Go in peace; keep warm and well fed," but does nothing about their physical needs, what good is it? In the same way, faith, if it is not accompanied by action, is dead."

Giving is predicated upon the greatest Giver of all times. This amazing act is beautifully expressed in the classic scripture, John 3:16 (NIV): "For God so loved the world that he gave his one and only Son, that whoever believes in him shall not perish but have eternal life." The ultimate sacrifice, the Lamb of God, is the most supreme Gift of all. Consequently, Jesus, the supreme Gift, has given ultimately of Himself. "He is our role model for sacrificial, joyful, and purposeful giving. No person has ever given as Jesus gave, for He gave His very life on the cross so that you and I might have eternal life. The person who operates in the motivational gift of giving has a tremendous opportunity to be a blessing to others, to encourage others in the proper use of their finances, and to make the extension of the Gospel possible."[20]

Motivational Tendencies

The seven motivational gifts of Romans 12 are practical in nature and describe the inner motivations of the Christian servant. These spiritual gifts produce certain motivating or influencing tendencies that drive how believers relate to others and to their surroundings. The Holy Spirit infuses every believer with qualities that shape their overall perspective on life. Because of this, those

---

20 Stanley, 2014.

with the gift of giving will find themselves unconsciously acting out specific inborn tendencies. This is an indication of our Creator's unique workmanship.

Givers have the capacity to serve God by sharing their material resources to further the work of the kingdom. They are thrifty spenders who constantly seek ways to save money. These individuals avoid lavish spending and save resources by making wise choices. They aim to glorify God by exercising wisdom and accountability in financial matters.

Have you been endowed with the gift of giving? Are you passionate about sharing your resources to meet the needs of others? Do you delight in finding less costly ways to conduct business transactions? Do you prefer to give anonymously to avoid recognition? Do you rarely incur debt?

As you continue in your quest to identify and confirm your gift(s), determine whether these motivational tendencies match your own. If they do, you are already reaping the joy that comes with such a beautiful ornament—the gift of giving. If the attributes listed do not reflect your motivational tendencies, I encourage you to continue seeking the Lord in the validation of your spiritual gift(s).

Let us observe what it is like to observe people and circumstances through the eyes of giving. The following list provides common attributes shared by those with this spiritual gift.

- Givers are passionate about sharing their financial assets as a means of honoring God. They have mastered the principle of Christian financial stewardship.

- Givers have an inherent nature that draws them to bless others financially. They unconsciously and voluntarily seek to meet specific needs.

- Givers may choose to contribute quietly or anonymously. Their desire is to glorify God through their gifts rather than to glorify themselves.

- Givers do not have to be coerced nor manipulated to give; instead, they are guided by an inner motivation to satisfy specific financial needs.

- Givers are characterized by their eagerness to give with joy and delight. Those who are endowed with this gift give willingly and cheerfully.

- Givers despise being pressured to satisfy random appeals. They may feel a deep repugnance for those who attempt to force or steer their giving.

- Givers are unrestrained in sharing their monetary resources. Rather than viewing their giving as a loss, they view it as a gain. They have gained their Lord's approval, which is their ultimate spiritual fulfillment.

- Givers are gratified as they meet financial needs overlooked by others.

- Givers are eager to contribute more than what is expected or required.

- Givers' motives for giving are pure. They do not seek prestige or prominence. In many instances, they are content with remaining anonymous.

- Givers search devoutly for opportunities to give.

- Givers contribute from their abundance as well as their lack.

- Givers are thrifty, prudent bargain hunters, but they offer qualitative gifts that are indicative of their standard of excellence.

- Givers expand their capacity to give by making wise investments.

- Givers courageously encourage and motivate others to give.

- Givers are unconsciously drawn to opportunities to contribute their financial resources.

- Givers have excellent money-management skills; they are very intuitive regarding money matters.

- Givers are not financially gullible; therefore, they are not easily tempted to compromise their integrity for material gain.

- Givers don't view tithing as giving 10 percent but as receiving 90 percent.

- Givers may miss Spirit-led opportunities to give to individuals or ministries. Once they encounter a single incident where their gift has been wasted or misused, they may refrain from giving altogether.

- Givers take joy in investing in the ministries or the lives of the recipients of their gifts. When they make a material contribution, they feel as if they are giving a part of themselves. Being part of another person's success brings joy to givers.[21]

- A Spirit-infused giver's motivation is to meet tangible needs by offering financial assistance. Givers love to share with others from the overflow of blessings God has given them. Because of this, they often adjust their lifestyle to contribute more to spreading of the gospel and caring for the needy.

3 *C's*—Characteristics, Challenges, and Choices

While each person in the body of Christ is unique, it is not unusual for those who operate in the same motivational gift to demonstrate common characteristics, to experience common challenges, and to serve in similar choices, or capacities in ministry.

Characteristics

While everyone in the body of Christ is unique, a believer who operates in the gift of giving may possess several of the following characteristics.

- An understanding that his or her giving glorifies God

- A generous and charitable nature

- Gives cheerfully and not grudgingly

- Is unconsciously drawn to people or causes that desire finances

---

21 Stanley, 2014.

- Sees giving as a personal investment in the lives and ministries of others

- Gives quietly or anonymously with no desire for recognition

- Gives to reflect quality rather than quantity

- Despises being pressured to satisfy random financial appeals

- Tends to contribute more than what is required

- Contributes out of his or her personal lack

- Is astute in financial and business matters

- Offers wise financial counsel

- Has excellent money-management skills

- Is conservative and thrifty; makes wise purchases

- Tends to save money, even when personal finances are strained

- Does not spend more than he or she makes and avoids debt

- Is considered by family members to be stingy

- Is considered by those who are recipients of contributions to be generous

- Searches diligently for wise financial investments

- Motivates others to give

- Is not financially gullible

Although each person's behavior will vary according to factors such as age, gender, culture, environment, background, temperament, and experiences, it is common for those who have the motivational gift of giving to demonstrate these characteristics.

Challenges

While everyone in the body of Christ is unique, a believer who operates in the gift of giving may encounter some of the following challenges.

- Uses his or her gifts to control lives and ministries

- May become zealous and overcommit at times

- Is critical of those who are not as willing to give

- Is forceful and sometimes pressures others to give

- Uses giving financially as a way to avoid other requirements

- Evaluates and devalues others' spirituality based on what they contribute

- Reflects "tunnel vision" as they focus on issues that they view as priorities

- Fails to acknowledge God's direction for giving as he or she succumbs to his or her interest

- Misses worthy opportunities to give as they reflect on past negative experiences

It is important that we acknowledge these challenges and pray diligently to overcome them. As we minister, God's purpose for spiritual gifts must always be in the forefront. He establishes a standard where spiritual gifts can operate in excellence.

Choices (Areas of Service)

While this list is not comprehensive, it can be used as a guide for directing those who are passionate about identifying and operating in their area of spiritual giftedness. The chart below provides the following: 1) suggested positions or areas of service, 2) descriptions of the positions or areas of service, 3) abilities and best personality traits for each position, and 4) the type of ministry or the specific group for whom the person is passionate about serving.[22]

"YOUR GIFT IS GOD'S GIFT TO YOU; WHAT YOU DO WITH IT IS YOUR GIFT TO GOD." ~ UNKNOWN

---

22 Gilbert and Spear, 2002.

Ministry Opportunities: Giving

Position	Description	Characteristics	Passionate About:
Financial Secretary	Responsible for keeping the church's financial records in accordance with legal, ethical, and biblical standards	*Abilities:* Some accounting education and background; good with figures; discreet; excellent organizational skills *Personality Traits:* Dependable, committed, and detail-oriented	Good stewardship and accuracy

| Financial Administrator | Helps provide accountability in the church through leading the development of the church's yearly budget and overseeing budget compliance | *Abilities:* Good organizational skills; experience in financial planning, accounting, or banking fields
Personality Traits: Dependable and analytical | Good financial management and accountability |
| Treasurer | Helps ensure ethical handling of all church funds and oversees management of church bank accounts | *Abilities:* Experience and/or education in the financial field
Personality Traits: Trustworthy, honest, sincere, and dependable | Good financial management and accountability |

This chart serves as a guide to help spiritually gifted givers identify opportunities. Here are other choices for ministering in this gift.

- Financial advisor or counselor

- Food and clothing distribution

- Emergency shelter

- Support groups

Other influencing factors drive a person's ability to minister, including age, level of spiritual maturity, and overall health (physical and emotional). I recommend that you collaborate with their local church leadership to develop your passions in ministry. Your spiritual advisors can help you select suitable options that are readily available within your local church.

In summary, believers with the gift of giving are motivated to give financial resources to satisfy tangible needs. Now that you have experienced what it's like to see life through the lenses of giving, you can develop a deeper appreciation for this gift.

Vision Enhancement

The motivational gifts function like a pair of eyeglasses, maximizing our spiritual vision. The gifts affect how we see life and respond to the needs around us. While prescriptive lenses correct or improve physical eyesight, these seven gifts alter or readjust spiritual sight. Like corrective lenses, as we "wear" these gifts, they serve as a remedy for impaired spiritual vision. They also influence our ability to focus on serving the body of Christ. To enhance physical vision, we must be willing to seek assistance in correcting our defective eyesight. The same is true of our spiritual vision. Consider physical nearsightedness and farsightedness. These are two common defects that can improve with proper intervention. Spiritual gifts can do the same thing for our spiritual vision.

- People who are spiritually nearsighted lack foresight and can only judge what is in front of them. Since such people are short-sighted, they cannot readily see distant images, which appear blurry. Visual accuracy is limited to only what is up close—the obvious.

- Spiritually farsighted individuals, on the other hand, can clearly see distant images, but objects that are in front of them appear blurry. Farsighted people can only judge images at a great distance.

Both visual impairments, nearsightedness and farsightedness, require prescriptive lenses for visual enhancement. It is amazing how these lenses help remedy both defects and improve overall vison. Likewise, if our spiritual eyesight is defective, we must be willing to receive the remedy that the Holy Spirit prescribes in the form of spiritual gifts.

Those who operate in the motivational gifts of the Spirit must clearly see people and circumstances through the lenses of their designated gifts. If we are to serve others in the body of Christ in an effective manner, our ability to focus on spiritual matters cannot be impaired. Believers who are spiritually nearsighted lack discretion in the things of God and cannot see the big picture. They are only capable of judging what is in front of them—the obvious. To nearsighted believers, any consideration outside of their apparent reach seems blurry. On the other hand, Christians who are spiritually farsighted tend to overlook what is directly in front of them.

In these instances, defective vision represents believers who misrepresent or abuse their spiritual gift(s), operating outside of their divine scope. Here is good news: both visual defects can be remedied. Almighty God, the Ultimate Designer, has provided corrective spiritual lenses that supersede those of any earthly optometrist.

Correcting Nearsightedness in Giving

Persons gifted in giving must be careful of becoming spiritually nearsighted, lacking foresight, and only judging what is in front of them. Here, nearsightedness symbolizes believers promoting their personal agenda or leaning toward their personal weaknesses, i.e., the challenges detailed in the previous section. Farsightedness, on the other hand, represents the giver's inability to acknowledge the needs of others. Givers must not become short-sighted, only focusing on self. Rather, givers must extend their spiritual vision further into the distance.

Givers exhibit nearsightedness when they allow a bitter incident from the past to influence their future decisions to contribute to worthy individuals or causes. Each person adorned with this gift will experience various forms of deception, disappointment, and disdain. These experiences may cause one to seriously regret extending a helping hand. It is quite disheartening to givers when their monetary contributions are misused or wasted. After all, as they financially contribute, they feel as though they are giving a part of themselves. When individuals, ministries, or other entities cross that line, givers feel violated. Not only do they view this misdeed as a personal offense, they are deeply pained because this abusive act dishonors God. Because they effortlessly exercise financial accountability, the thought of their contribution being wasted is heartbreaking.

During such times, givers' spiritual sensitivity diminishes, and their focus begins to shift. They become fixated on the close and obvious—their immediate feelings of mounting regret. This nearsightedness impairs their spiritual vision. A giver's visual capability should extend beyond the obvious. It should expand to more distant images, which is symbolic of the ongoing financial needs of various individuals, ministries, and causes.

This defective vision must be corrected immediately. Givers should never allow any circumstance to disrupt their ministry or allow any concern to distract their focus. Spiritual gifts should be exercised to bring glory to the Creator. God designed the workings of these gifts to edify or to build up the members of His church. When a believer fails to exhibit Christian virtues, his or her spiritual gift fails to yield fruit. It also creates an entry for the flow of criticism and skepticism from spectators. Other believers may begin to doubt the giver's motives. This is detrimental to the overall effectiveness of ministry. For this reason, givers must not succumb to their carnal nature. They must not give in to their fleshly desires or emotions. Instead, Christians with this gift must maintain a healthy spiritual life. A daily regimen consisting of Bible study and prayer sets the tone for a proper balance.

Givers must position themselves to receive divine guidance for giving. A dampened spirit can be revived by the Master's touch. As givers' spiritual sensitivity is heightened, they hear from God and begin to alter their ill feelings. They prayerfully reconnect to their purpose and resume their passion to exalt the Lord through their special gift. Givers are spiritually rejuvenated as they rediscover their dedication to contribute as the Holy Spirit guides. The Spirit of God reassures those with the gift of giving, as referenced in Proverbs 11:25 (NIV): "a generous person will prosper; whoever refreshes others will be refreshed." Furthermore, the bitter experiences with past recipients create an opportunity for spiritual growth and maturation. Givers acquire wisdom and insight from these experiences that they can apply to future decision-making. When this occurs, they can magnify the Lord through unrestrained Spirit-infused giving.

Correcting Farsightedness in Giving

Givers must also be careful of becoming spiritually farsighted. Focusing primarily on distant images or the big picture may cause them to miss the obvious—what is directly in front of them. Givers may be driven only to see images in the distance, such as the impact of their substantial financial contribution to a prestigious project. This farsightedness is reflected by an overzealousness to be associated with such a distinguished cause. In the process, givers may be accused of using their gifts to control people or certain aspects of the project. They may adopt an attitude that totally disregards other key individuals. Farsighted givers only judge images at a distance: the influence of their contributions. The objects that are directly in front of them can become quite blurry. These objects represent the feelings and emotions of other individuals involved in the combined effort. If this happens, it is imperative that givers rediscover their original objective for contributing.

This impaired vision, farsightedness, can be corrected as givers focus on the obvious—exercising humility and treating others fairly. As disciples of Christ, we must always exhibit courtesy and kindness while exercising our spiritual gifts. The Holy Spirit endows us to minister effectively to His church with a heavenly graceful flavor—love. The supremacy of love must always overrule our desire to offend. When we lean toward a carnal focus, Christ's ministry becomes compromised, which may lead others to discredit the gifts and bypass the benefits that they provide. As we stand on the pillar of Philippians 4:13, we can overcome all challenges through Christ, who gives us strength. Furthermore, it is futile to even attempt to exercise a spiritual gift without blending it with genuine affection and consideration of others. The apostle Paul eloquently expresses this spiritual truth in 1 Corinthians 13:1 (NIV), "If I speak in the tongues of men and angels, but do not have love, I am only a resounding gong or a clanging cymbal."

Givers must further realize that giving is a privilege. It is not a chess piece that they can move recklessly from square to square to capture something. Rather, the gift of giving is a divine impartation where those who receive it readily give their financial resources without any ulterior motives. Givers who are in fellowship with the Lord will not seek to glorify themselves; on the contrary, they diligently give of their resources to exalt the name of Jesus, our Lord.

Vision Maintenance

Maintaining optimum spiritual vision is crucial. Once we are suitably matched to our Designer's eyewear, we must strive to keep them looking like new. Our spiritual lenses should remain free of spots and smears that can affect our focus. Spots and smears may symbolize the marring effects of our gifts if we become distracted. For example, distractions in the form of gifts that you don't possess but are attempting to operate in are like a spot or a smear. We must do whatever it takes to remove these smudges by reattaching to our God-infused spiritual gift, thereby enhancing our spiritual focus.

We must be intentional when it comes to maintaining and enhancing our visual health. The Ultimate Designer, through His Son, Jesus, set the example of how to boost spiritual vision. He engaged in spiritual disciplines such as study, meditation, prayer (solitude and silence), fasting, worship, service, and fellowship with other believers. Likewise, our spiritual vision will be enhanced as we practice the following.

- Study—Read and study God's Word for guidance and direction.

- Meditate—Ponder God's Word to maintain spiritual focus.

- Pray—Commune with God (solitude) and listen to Him (silence).

- Fast—Abstain from food or other distractors for a designated period.

- Worship—Engage in private and corporate worship, which connects us to God.

- Serve—Assist others compassionately, as Jesus did.

- Fellowship—Interact with other believers for encouragement and to equip each other for service.

As we engage in these maintenance practices, we will achieve the Designer's fashionable look. In addition, our vision will be remarkably enhanced, and our spiritual focus will be maximized. We will see objects at any distance, for we will have been fitted with the Ultimate Designer's eyewear. While optometrists utilize digital measurements to ensure an accurate and precise prescription, the Ultimate Designer operates with a precision that is unmatchable.

Finally, the gift of giving is a unique adornment assigned by the Holy Spirit. Once believers receive confirmation of this gift, they will seek to achieve clearer vision through the lens of the cross. Jesus, the Anointed One, will be their focal point and example as they exercise this spiritual gift in love and faithfulness. As they fully trust God, the Ultimate Designer, and wear the lenses of giving, they will minister with a touch of grace. The Holy Spirit has assigned the eyewear of giving to enhance spiritual vision by adding or subtracting focusing power to the lives of believers. I have shared several guarantees that accompany this corrective remedy. The spiritual lenses of giving prescribed by the Holy Spirit are:

- Progressive—they enable us to see both near and far

- Shatterproof—they are reliable and unbreakable

- Impact-resistant—they can withstand any opposing or colliding force

- Scratch-resistant—they cannot be scratched or damaged

In addition, the frames attached to these spiritual lenses have the following features:

- Spring-loaded—they are less likely to be bent or warped

- Silicone Nose Pads—they prevent the eyeglasses from slipping

- Straps—they hold the glasses firmly in place

Congratulations! You have experienced spiritual eyesight through the lenses of giving. Your knowledge and appreciation of this gift have been expanded. Since it is imperative that you identify, cultivate, and operate in your assigned gifts (1 Pet. 4:10; 1 Cor. 12 and 14), I encourage you to prayerfully confirm and validate your divine endowment. Discovering and confirming your spiritual gifts will help you remain in your ministry lane, thereby avoiding a head-on collision.

Can you confirm that giving is your ministry passion? If so, praise the Lord for adorning you with such a precious ornament—the gift of giving. I encourage you to continue to seek the Lord in the cultivation and operation of your divine gift. If you need further guidance in identifying your gift, prayerfully navigate through the following chapters, and continue to review the remaining motivational gifts of the Spirit for identification and confirmation.

The Gifted Believer's Prayer:

Father, how excellent is Your name in all the earth. Your name is worthy of all glory and honor. Today I confess my sins and bind myself to godly repentance. Almighty God, from the fruit of my lips, I offer thanksgiving to you, for I appreciate this precious gift of giving. I treasure your Word, for it is perfect and complete. As I yield myself to giving, let my deeds of kindness and benevolence bring joy to all recipients. Enrich me in all things and in every way, so I can be a wise and generous giver. Amen.

CHAPTER 6

Through the Lenses
of Leadership

> "If it is to lead, do it diligently."
> ~ Romans 12:8 (NIV)

Just as prescriptive lenses improve physical vision, the motivational spiritual gifts of Romans 12 enhance our spiritual vision. Each gift functions like a pair of lenses, sharpening our spiritual focus as we serve others in the body of Christ. These gifts are frequently cited as "motivational gifts" because they are practical in nature and describe the inner motivations of gifted believers. Each believer has inherent motivational tendencies that drive the way he or she responds to various circumstances. The spiritual gifts affect how we see life and respond to the needs around us. As the Ultimate Designer, the Holy Spirit infuses each of us with a customized spiritual gift, which allows us to see people and circumstances through a specific set of lenses that remedy our impaired vision.

The Designer's Eyewear promotes godly and righteous living as a prerequisite for operating in the seven areas of spiritual giftedness. In the prelude to Romans 12, the apostle Paul urged the church in Rome to present their bodies as living sacrifices (12:1–2). He went on to urge them to offer humble service in the body of Christ (12:3). In addition, regenerated believers will also possess the fruit of the Spirit of Galatians 5:22–23—love, joy, peace, longsuffering, gentleness, goodness, faith, meekness, and temperance. Accordingly, as Spirit-filled believers wear the Designer's prescriptive lenses or spiritual eyewear, their vision will align more closely with how God views the world.

This book is based on the presumption that love conquers all. Immediately following the list of spiritual gifts, the apostle Paul further challenged the church to translate love into action (Rom. 12:9–21). He emphasized the sincerity, devotion, zeal, fervor, joy, compassion, and empathy demonstrated through genuine love. True disciples of Christ will exhibit love when operating in their spiritual giftedness. The supremacy of love always overrules the desire to disrupt the flow of the church's mission. We should never allow spiritual giftings to supersede Christian character. On the contrary, character should rise to the forefront while the gifting lags slightly. It is futile to attempt to exercise a spiritual gift without blending it with genuine affection and consideration of others. The apostle Paul eloquently expresses this spiritual truth in 1 Corinthians 13:1 (NIV): "If I speak in the tongues of men and angels, but do not have love, I am only a resounding gong or a clanging cymbal." *The Designer's Eyewear* is written with the notion that each spiritual gift is implemented and aligned with God's Word.

Gift Overview

The Ultimate Designer, God Almighty, is dedicated to presenting various options and exclusives in designer eyewear just for you. In this chapter, I present one of the seven options, the sixth motivational spiritual gift of Romans 12, the gift of leadership. As with the other spiritual gifts, the Holy Spirit assigns this gift to certain believers. It is a supernatural gift that enables recipients to lead others in meaningful endeavors. This gift is coupled with a demonstration of Christian compassion, which is essential to empowering others and encouraging spiritual growth. Leaders are to take charge of their work with constant diligence. This involves watching over the body of believers to which they are assigned and demonstrating a readiness to sacrifice personal comfort for the benefit of their followers. The Holy Spirit infuses some with the spiritual gift of leadership to care for God's people and lead them into deeper relationships with Christ and with each other.

Spiritually gifted leaders prayerfully steer groups of believers from disorder to order—from disorganization to organization (cf. 1 Cor. 14:33, NLT). This is prayerfully conducted through the implementation of the following: organizational structure, motivational techniques, strategic planning, and diligent execution. Leaders may be characterized as "movers and shakers" who are influential and persuasive, bold and uninhibited. These unique attributes are not driven by a personal quest for prestige or prominence. Instead, believers with this gift are motivated to provide credible leadership that honors God. Such people thrive when given the green light to move forward with competency exhibited by leadership expertise. They waste no time implementing a plan, whether pre-determined or spontaneous, to arouse and coordinate the actions of others. Their sharp spiritual discernment equips them to identify spiritual gifts, talents, skills, and abilities in others that are needed to perform worthy spiritual endeavors.

Even amid a world plagued with increasing chaos and complexities, everything rises and falls on leadership. However, numerous misconceptions are associated with this gift. Let us examine two false perceptions about the spiritual gift of leadership. There are those who believe that the gift is driven primarily by human will. This view is based on biased thinking and lack of understanding. Another perception is that leaders who gravitate towards loyal followers are guilty of demonstrating favoritism. Neither of these perspectives can be biblically substantiated.

The gift of leadership, contrary to popular thought, is not fueled by human will. This gift, as with the other spiritual gifts, is driven instead by our Creator's divine will. It is a Spirit-generated endowment assigned to certain believers. Spiritually gifted leaders are often misunderstood in their attempts to honor God through effective leadership. They are mistakenly viewed as strong-willed, controlling individuals who desire to take over, manipulate, and disrupt the status quo. Too often, believers fail to acknowledge that order, structure, and organization originate with God. These three components are not random items that leaders decide to include on a wish list. They are legitimate pieces that must be added to the overall puzzle to extinguish chaos and confusion. Several accounts in scripture unveil God's divine position on establishing and maintaining order. Let us examine two of the more notable ones.

We can easily observe the inception of order in the Creation account, Genesis 1–2. The world was created in a precise, sequential, organized manner. It has been stated that "earth is not the product of a series of cosmic accidents, nor is humanity the result of a million-year happenstance evolution."[23] God, in His omnipotence, developed a precise order for the creation of a physical environment and the filling of that environment. He formed creation in an orderly manner from nothing in six literal, twenty-four-hour periods:

- Day 1 — The heavens and the earth

- Day 2 — The sky

- Day 3 — Dry land

- Day 4 — The stars and the heavenly bodies

- Day 5 — All that lives in the water

- Day 6 — All creatures that live on dry land, including humans

God's creative work was complete at the end of the sixth day, and He rested on the seventh day. Again, the orderly inception of the universe is displayed through the unveiling of this timeline of events. In addition to the creation account, God's hand can also be observed in the orderly establishment of the family, the church, the state, and even in the regulation of the economy (Ex. 23:3–19). The implementation of leadership is driven by God's divine will.

1 Corinthians 14:40 (NIV) declares, "Let all things be done decently and in order." Though this verse provides guidance for orderly utterance of prayer and praise in public worship, the underlining spiritual principle is relevant to all aspects of

---

23 Walter J. Veith, "Understanding the Creation Week," *amazingdiscoveries. org,* last visited April 29, 2020, https://amazingdiscoveries.org/C-deception-Creation_week_evolution.

ministry. This ruling is still applicable as we promote and sustain ministries in the body of Christ. The theory and practice of decency and order is vitally important to the church's edification and spiritual growth. Accordingly, effective spiritual leadership extinguishes chaos, confusion, noise, and disorderly conduct. In addition, the local church must gain clarity in defining roles and responsibilities, ministries and missions, operations, and other aspects of ministry. As this occurs, the Christian assembly will reflect methodical leadership. The spiritual gift of leadership, when exercised accordingly, creates a culture marked by decent and orderly management.

Another misconception is that the leader who gravitates to a specific individual or group of individuals is guilty of demonstrating favoritism. Quite often, spiritually gifted leaders are accused of being cliquish, attaching themselves to members of an exclusive group. As it relates to church affairs, there is a distinction between the formation of a clique and the formation of an inner circle. A clique denotes a small group with common interests that does not readily allow others to join. An inner circle denotes a small group with common interests that encourages others to join them. While the foundational core of a clique is strife and competition, an inner circle is built upon the premise of Christian maturity and loyalty. Since the people closest to us determine our level of achievement, leaders must surround themselves with loyal, competent individuals. They subconsciously gravitate toward those who demonstrate loyalty to God first, followed by loyalty to the leader. These trusted individuals constitute the leader's inner circle. Spiritually gifted leaders understand that their success centers upon what can be accomplished through others and not merely what they can achieve on their own. Leaders are drawn to those who demonstrate an interest in the work of the kingdom as well as those who have special abilities and skills that promote the ministry. Accordingly, they welcome others to join them in carrying out Christ's mandates.

Let us further review the principle of the inner circle, as it relates to Moses and Jesus. The great patriarch, Moses, implemented the principle of the inner circle, as recorded in Deuteronomy 1:6–18. Through the act of delegation (verses 9–12), Moses "chose to set his ego aside and share his leadership responsibilities with others. He would give them both the responsibility and authority to do the work; the task now became a team effort."[24] Furthermore, Moses exhibited exceptional leadership skills (verses 13–15) in the selection of his inner circle. "Moses chose his inner circle from among the spiritually qualified, approved, and appointed according to their abilities."[25] It may have appeared to some that Moses demonstrated favoritism in this selection; however, his criteria and approval for leadership was based upon his team's loyalty to God first, followed by his loyalty to them.

As we follow the life and ministry of Jesus, it is obvious that He had a group of loyal followers. Jesus, the greatest Leader of all times, most effectively implemented the principle of the inner circle in the selection and dispatching of the twelve apostles. The Master Teacher selected each of these servants for a specific purpose. As Christians, we hold these men (excluding Judas Iscariot) in high esteem for their divine mission—to travel, eat, and live with Jesus, experiencing firsthand His life and ministry. While Jesus had an inner circle (twelve apostles), He encouraged them to invite others to join. He and His inner circle turned the world upside down, as referenced in Acts 17:6.

---

24 John C. Maxwell, *The Maxwell Leadership Bible* (Nashville: Thomas Nelson, 2019), page number.
25 Ibid.

Jesus expanded the principle of the inner circle as he relied heavily upon three aspiring spiritual giants within His immediate circle—Peter, James, and John. These three men are recognized as Christ's inner circle. While it is not clear why Jesus handpicked these three, it is evident that He held them in high esteem and wanted them to acquire a higher level of spiritual consciousness. Peter, James, and John were called out for special elevation. After all, the threesome was chosen to be present at the following major events while the other apostles were not.

- *The Transfiguration.* This event involved the "glorification of the human body of Jesus."[26] Jesus allowed Peter, James, and John to accompany Him to a high mountain, where He was transfigured. Jesus became radiant in glory, and a grand series of appearances and events followed. Jesus's Sonship was clearly confirmed as God declared, "This is my beloved Son, in whom I am well pleased" (Matt. 7:1–8; Mk. 9:2–8; Lk. 9:28–36, NIV).

- *The Healing of the Damsel.* Jesus allowed no one to follow Him except Peter, James, and John as they entered Jairus' home to restore life to the ruler's young daughter. The three were overcome with amazement as they witnessed this explosive miracle (Mk. 5:37–42).

- *The Gethsemane Experience.* As Jesus's earthly mission reached an end, He commanded His disciples to sit and wait while He addressed Peter, James, and John privately. This occurred during the Lord's final agonizing hours as He prayed in the Garden of Gethsemane.

---

26 Don Stewart, "What Was the Significance of Jesus' Transfiguration?", *Blue Letter Bible,* last visited April 29, 2020, https://www.blueletterbible.org/faq/don_stewart/don_stewart_786.cfm.

It is a privilege to be called to provide leadership in the body of Christ. The gift of leadership is not an arbitrary calling; it should never be based on favoritism, seniority, nepotism, random choices, or personal whims. Instead, the selection process for leaders should be guided by scripture. Contrary to popular belief, an individual should not be assigned to lead a group of believers simply because he or she desires to do so. A desire to lead should never be the rule of thumb. After all, a believer's behavioral tendencies are connected to the gifting that the Holy Spirit has assigned. Operating in our assigned gifting is essential to our service to God. It helps us determine where to focus our time and effort for the greatest impact in God's kingdom. Church leaders are responsible to ensure that members serve in God-ordained areas of ministry. God holds the church in high esteem; after all, "the church is His Body, His Bride, His Army and His Family."[27] According to Ephesians 4:13 (ESV), the goal of spiritually gifted leaders is to guard and guide those they lead "until we all attain to the unity of the faith and of the knowledge of the Son of God, to mature manhood, to the measure of the stature of the fullness of Christ."

Leadership in the New Testament

The New Testament contains numerous examples of exceptional leadership. The following passages provide several biblical models of leadership.

- The apostle Paul, a leader committed to a specific, meaningful mission, had an apostolic assignment to preach among the Gentiles (Acts 13:47, KJV).

---

27 Darrell W. Johnson, "Biblical Requirements of Leaders," *Christianity Today,* last accessed April 29, 2020, https://www.christianitytoday.com/pastors/2007/july-online-only/le-040329.html.

- Peter, an impulsive leader and often a spokesperson for the other apostles, bounced back after several downfalls (Matt. 14:30 KJV; Matt. 16:22–23, KJV; Matt. 26:74, KJV; Acts 2:14, 41).

- Barnabas, a great arbitrator who survived the opposition of differing opinions, modeled how opposing sides should respect each other (Acts 15:1–21; Gal. 2:1–10, KJV).

The gift of leadership is also expressed as the "gift of ruling" in Romans 12:8 (KJV).

The most profound leader of all time is Jesus, the Redeemer of humankind. His earthly ministry was nothing less than transformational as He led numerous individuals in meaningful endeavors. Today, Jesus, through the Holy Spirit, is still empowering, instructing, inspiring, rebuking, and comforting us. He has saved, healed, and delivered us from spiritual and temporal ailments that would have otherwise destroyed us. These actions constitute effective leadership.

As a true leader, Jesus had compassion for others. He demonstrated a readiness to sacrifice personal comfort for the benefit of His followers. The entire Gospel—the life, death, burial, and resurrection of Christ—reflects His countless sacrificial acts of service. He left us a blueprint for leadership—instructing, inspiring, and encouraging while offering an unmatchable gift, the gift of salvation.

Motivational Tendencies

The seven motivational gifts of Romans 12 are practical in nature and describe the inner motivations of the Christian servant. These spiritual gifts produce certain motivating or influencing tendencies that drive how we relate to others and to our surroundings. The Holy Spirit infuses us with qualities that shape our overall perspective on life. Because of this, we will find ourselves unconsciously acting out specific inborn tendencies. This is an indication of our Creator's unique workmanship.

People gifted in leadership are motivated to prescribe order while deflecting chaos. Persevering comes easily for spiritually gifted leaders, for their vision is ignited by a fuming passion. They exhibit unwavering faith and declare ultimate victory before reaching the finish line. Believers with this gift maneuver with a great expectation, believing God to perform what others deem impossible. They are elated about steering their followers toward godly goals and actions. Such leaders' outstanding traits make their leadership look quite attractive.

Have you been endowed with the gift of leadership? Are you a self-starter? Do you find yourself subconsciously identifying resources needed to jump-start a project? Do you feel restless or frustrated when things are disorderly? Perhaps you find yourself delegating duties or tasks with ease. Are you one who can receive criticism without crumbling? Do you have the knack for selecting and assigning the right people to the right jobs?

As you continue in your quest to identify and confirm your gift, determine whether these motivational tendencies match your own. If they do, then you are already reaping the joy that comes with such a beautiful ornament—the gift of leadership. If the attributes listed do not reflect your motivational tendencies, I encourage you to continue seeking the Lord in the validation of your spiritual gift(s).

Let us observe what it is like to view people and circumstances through the lenses of a spiritually gifted leader. The following list provides descriptions common to those who are endowed with this gift.

- Spiritually gifted leaders exhibit unwavering faith in God's ability to perform the impossible. They are baffled by other believers' lack of faith in accomplishing specific goals. Such leaders are wired in a way that reflects a can-do rather than a "can't-do" approach. This is one reason why these spiritual achievers meet and exceed their goals.

- Spiritually gifted leaders are bold and courageous. As others succumb to fear and doubt, they accept challenges and move forward with zeal and anticipation.

- Spiritually gifted leaders are visionaries who can see the big picture. They are skillful in visualizing the outcome of a major undertaking prior to its completion. Their relentless faith drives them to strive for goals that others deem unattainable. God has spiritually equipped these leaders to see the big picture clearly while most of their followers see it quite dimly or not at all.

- Spiritually gifted leaders are effective communicators. They motivate and persuade others to act upon what they present. This is essential to vision casting or the flowing down of the vision to their followers. True leaders receive God-given dreams and skillfully communicate specific aspects to their followers. When those following understand and embrace the vision, there is mutual buy-in. As a result, leaders transcend into a role of influence and inspiration.

- Spiritually gifted leaders are skillful in creating long-term goals; however, they can also dissect a complicated project, thereby breaking it down into achievable short-term goals. They break seemingly impossible tasks into smaller units that can be easily managed. This way, their followers can work toward smaller goals and experience iterations of success as they move toward the bigger picture.

- Spiritually gifted leaders are self-starters. They do not depend on another person's spark to "light them up." Instead, they light the fire themselves. They jump into a project with little or no coercion.

- Spiritually gifted leaders are skillful in identifying the resources—both people and material resources—necessary to accomplish a goal. As soon as they are directed toward a goal, such leaders subconsciously lay out a mental picture before attempting to put a plan on paper. Their intuitive nature automatically kicks into operation as they roll out a slate of resources that can be used.

- Spiritually gifted leaders empower others by delegating responsibilities. They fully understand that their success centers upon what can be accomplished through others and not merely upon what they can achieve on their own. They have no desire to receive all the credit or accolades.

- Spiritually gifted leaders rejoice at the completion of a task. Although they may not physically perform the task, they make sure the job gets done through organization and delegation.

- Spiritually gifted leaders can receive criticism without dismantling. Because their position of authority places them at the forefront, they understand that their role is often accompanied by criticism, blame, and misunderstandings. Nevertheless, leaders will not break down nor fall apart when others condemn or attack them.

- Spiritually gifted leaders expect loyalty from their followers. They are subconsciously drawn to those who demonstrate loyalty to God first, followed by loyalty to the leader. These trusted followers constitute the leader's inner circle.

- Spiritually gifted leaders gravitate to those who demonstrate an interest in the work of the kingdom as well as those who have special abilities and skills that promote the ministry. This attraction is sometimes misinterpreted as favoritism.

- Spiritually gifted leaders naturally assume leadership amid disorder. Their tendency to lead becomes stimulated under certain circumstances. When a spiritually gifted leader is placed amidst a culture characterized by disorganization, their leadership skills emerge. As a result, they subconsciously begin to do what God has gifted them to do. Some misinterpret this as the leader "taking over" or desiring to be in control, but it is merely an outworking of their spiritual gift.

- Spiritually gifted leaders are not motivated by cheers from the sidelines, applause, or monetary rewards. Instead, they receive deep satisfaction in knowing that a goal has been accomplished in a manner that is pleasing to God.

Do you recognize any of these traits within yourself? If not, then perhaps you've observed a number of these exhibited by other believers. Either way, you are now on your way to gaining further insight into the common traits associated with the gift of leadership.

These characterizations give credence to the motivation of leadership, to steer a group of believers from disorder to order, from disorganization to organization. Individuals gifted in leadership have a deep sense of conviction, driven by a passion to lead God's people into a meaningful relationship with Christ and one other. They honor God through effective leadership. Now that you've experienced sight through the lenses of leadership, you can develop a keener appreciation for this gift as well as for others who serve in this ministry capacity.

3 *C's*—Characteristics, Challenges, and Choices

While each person in the body of Christ is unique, it is not unusual for those who operate in the same motivational gift to demonstrate common characteristics, to experience common challenges, and to serve in similar choices, or capacities in ministry.

Characteristics

While everyone in the body of Christ is unique, a believer who operates in the gift of leadership may possess several of the following characteristics.

- Is influential, persuasive, and inspiring

- Is a courageous self-starter

- Is an effective communicator

- Has exceptional people skills

- Delegates responsibilities

- Dislikes mundane routine

- Readily gives credit to others

- Delights in the completion of tasks

- Thrives when given authority to lead

- Possesses exceptional organizational skills

- Sacrifices personal comfort to benefit others

- Readily identifies resources needed to complete a task

- Endures criticism while focusing on the tasks at hand

- Gravitates toward individuals who demonstrate loyalty

- Is a visionary—sees the big picture when others do not

- Demonstrates a can-do rather than a can't-do approach

- Discerns strengths, weaknesses, and abilities in others and matches them to tasks accordingly.

Although each person's behavior will vary according to factors such as age, gender, culture, environment, background, temperament, and experiences, it is common for those who have the motivational gift of leadership to demonstrate the above charactcristics.

Challenges

While everyone in the body of Christ is unique, a believer who operates in the gift of leadership may encounter one or more of the following challenges.

- Uses delegation to avoid work

- Is not responsive to directions from others

- Coerces others to achieve their own personal ambitions

- Gives instructions without clear explanations

- Fails to communicate vision effectively to others

- Does not readily offer praises or commendations

- Neglects family due to love of work

- Becomes callous due to constant criticism

- Comes off as bossy or controlling

- Puts project goals ahead of people's feelings

- Dismisses character flaws in others, focusing instead on their skills, talents, and special abilities

It is important that we recognize and acknowledge all these challenges and pray diligently to overcome each. We must recognize that spiritual gifts are assigned by the Holy Spirit to equip us to benefit others and to glorify God. These special endowments also serve the purpose of revealing the Living God to non-believers. Our Heavenly Father strategically established a standard where spiritual gifts can operate in excellence. When spiritually gifted leaders lean toward a carnal or selfish focus, Christ's ministry becomes compromised, which may lead others to dishonor the gifts and consequently bypass the benefits they provide.

Choices (Areas of Service):

While this list is not comprehensive, it can be used as a guide for directing those who are passionate about identifying and operating in their area of spiritual giftedness. The chart below provides the following: 1) suggested positions or areas of service, 2) descriptions of the positions or areas of service, 3) abilities and best personality traits for each position, and 4) the type of ministry or the specific group for whom the person is passionate about serving.[28]

> "YOUR GIFT IS GOD'S GIFT TO YOU; WHAT YOU
> DO WITH IT IS YOUR GIFT TO GOD."
> ~ UNKNOWN

---

28 Gilbert and Spear, 2002.

Ministry Opportunities: Leadership

Position	Description	Characteristics	Passionate About:
Building and Grounds Administrator	Responsible for the general upkeep and oversight of the church property and supervision of the church custodian	*Abilities:* General construction, building maintenance, lawncare skills, and the ability to supervise others *Personality Traits:* Dependable, hard-working, initiative to get things done without direct supervision, dependable	Good stewardship of the facilities God has given the church; presenting a positive physical appearance of the church to the community
Director of Operations	Provides vision and directional leadership for all operations staff, ministries, and volunteers	*Abilities:* Administrative skills, technical skills, communication skills, mitigation skills *Personality Traits:* Dependable, detail-oriented, expressive, and analytical	The growth and development of the local church and the wider Kingdom of God

Youth Director	Plans and oversees programs and activities for children and youth at a church or community outreach organization	*Abilities:* Good organizational and planning skills; good communicator; ability to motivate and inspire *Personality Traits:* Dependable, friendly, and expressive	Influencing and affecting young people's lives with the gospel of Christ

This chart serves as a guide in helping leaders identify opportunities for serving. Here are additional positions or areas of service a person gifted in leadership may consider.

- Church planter

- Consultant

- Leader of any ministry

- Overseer

- Pastor

- Researcher

- Strategic planner

- Trainer

Other influencing factors drive a person's ability to minister, including age, level of spiritual maturity, and overall health (physical and emotional). I recommend that you collaborate with their local church leadership to develop your passions in ministry. Your spiritual advisors can assist you in selecting suitable options that are readily available within the local church.

In summary, believers gifted in leadership are motivated to help others work together to achieve desired goals. Now that you have experienced what life looks like through the lenses of leadership, you can develop a deeper appreciation for this gift.

Vision Enhancement

The motivational gifts function like a pair of eyeglasses, maximizing our spiritual vision. The gifts affect how we see life and respond to the needs around us. While prescriptive lenses correct or improve physical eyesight, these seven gifts alter or readjust spiritual sight. Like corrective lenses, as we "wear" these gifts, they serve as a remedy for impaired spiritual vision. They also influence our ability to focus on serving the body of Christ. To enhance physical vision, we must be willing to seek assistance in correcting our defective eyesight. The same is true of our spiritual vision. Consider physical nearsightedness and farsightedness. These are two common defects that can improve with proper intervention. Spiritual gifts can do the same thing for our spiritual vision.

- People who are spiritually nearsighted lack foresight and can only judge what is in front of them. Since such people are short-sighted, they cannot readily see distant images, which appear blurry. Visual accuracy is limited to only what is up close—the obvious.

- Spiritually farsighted individuals, on the other hand, can clearly see distant images, but objects that are in front of them appear blurry. Farsighted people can only judge images at a great distance.

Both visual impairments, nearsightedness and farsightedness, require prescriptive lenses for visual enhancement. It is amazing how these lenses help remedy both defects and improve overall vison. Likewise, if our spiritual eyesight is defective, we must be willing to receive the remedy that the Holy Spirit prescribes in the form of spiritual gifts.

Those who operate in the motivational gifts of the Spirit must clearly see people and circumstances through the lenses of their designated gifts. If we are to serve others in the body of Christ in an effective manner, our ability to focus on spiritual matters cannot be impaired. Believers who are spiritually nearsighted lack discretion in the things of God and cannot see the big picture. They are only capable of judging what is in front of them—the obvious. To nearsighted believers, any consideration outside of their apparent reach seems blurry. On the other hand, Christians who are spiritually farsighted tend to overlook what is directly in front of them.

In these instances, defective vision represents believers who misrepresent or abuse their spiritual gift(s), operating outside of their divine scope. Here is good news: both visual defects can be remedied. Almighty God, the Ultimate Designer, has provided corrective spiritual lenses that supersede those of any earthly optometrist.

Correcting Nearsightedness in Leadership

Persons gifted in leadership must strive to avoid becoming spiritually nearsighted, lacking foresight, and only judging what is in front of them. Here, nearsightedness symbolizes leaders promoting their personal agenda or leaning toward their personal weaknesses, i.e., the challenges detailed in the previous section. Farsightedness, on the other hand, represents the spiritually gifted leader's inability to acknowledge the needs of others. Leaders must not become short-sighted, focusing only on self-fulfillment. Instead, leaders must extend their spiritual vision into the distance. They must provide sharp oversight over any undertaking. This includes exercising discernment in balancing a group's skills, talents, and special abilities with their personalities, characters, and maturity level.

Spiritually gifted leaders should never compromise the integrity of God's work. While selecting highly skilled team members is essential to a project's success, it is equally important to select those who possess godly character. When a leader chooses to overlook a team member's foul attitude simply because that person is skillful, that leader has resorted to a trade-off. He or she has made a situational decision to trade a significant quality (godly character) in return for gaining something lesser. This is a clear example of nearsightedness. Such leaders lack foresight and can only judge what is in front of them.

Since such individuals are short-sighted, they cannot readily see distant images—these images appear blurry. Again, visual accuracy is limited to only what is obvious, matching highly skilled people to vacant positions. When rancid attitudes go unchecked, conflicts arise, and dissention heightens. As a result, the group's momentum falters. It is certainly demotivating to work alongside an individual who demonstrates spiritual immaturity. As the toxic team member blatantly disregards others, a hostile work environment develops. If the leader fails to address this distraction, an emotional eruption may occur. Conversely, onlookers may begin to focus more on the troublemaker rather than gleaning from the spiritual experience. In this case, a deed that was intended to be spiritually fruitful becomes tainted and unfruitful.

Spiritually gifted leaders should never become so focused on someone's outstanding skills that they dismiss the person's ungodly behavior. People gifted in leadership must see beyond the obvious and be willing to extend their vision into the distance and value godly character above all else. This involves sharpening their sense of discernment and adjusting the group's demographics. Spiritually gifted leaders who are operating in holiness understand that their exceptional abilities are supernatural, and that God can accomplish more with less. In other words, God can maximize the performance of less-skillful but more spiritually mature believers, to the point it will outshine the performance of immature, more-skillful believers.

Finally, spiritually gifted leaders aim to honor the Lord by demonstrating effective leadership. Their defective vision must be corrected. Their visual accuracy should go beyond the obvious—nearsightedness—and extend to distant images. Many leaders can see what is obvious—recruiting highly skilled people to perform specific duties—but distant images are often blurry. Instead, spiritually gifted leaders must strive to envision distant images that symbolize and recognize godly character.

Correcting Farsightedness in Leadership

Leaders must also be careful of becoming spiritually farsighted. Focusing primarily on distant images or the big picture may cause them to miss the obvious—what is directly in front of them.

Here, farsightedness represents the visionary leader's insight. Leaders may be driven only to see images in the distance—the outcome of that prestigious project—without considering what is right in front of them, their capacity to communicate the vision effectively.

When spiritually gifted leaders receive a vision, they undergo a series of steps: they conceptualize it, visualize it, communicate it, and then they facilitate it. In their zeal to obtain rapid results, they may neglect to communicate fundamental details. While leaders are prone to seeing the big picture (distant images), they must recognize that their followers see it quite dimly or not at all. A spiritually gifted leader's ability to provide clear directions and to offer clarity is essential to the success of any undertaking. If the leader's primary focus is the resulting outcome, and they neglect to provide clear instructions, their followers may become disenchanted, disengaged, and/or demotivated. When the momentum of a project is compromised, skillful followers may be tempted to abandon the effort. If this happens, the group's dynamics begin to shift, and the outcome may be devastating.

As an effective communicator, spiritually gifted leaders are positioned to motivate and to persuade others to take action. This is especially essential to vision casting or the flowing down of the vision from leader to followers. When gifted leaders receive God-given dreams and aspirations, they skillfully disseminate detailed information to their followers. As the recipients begin to comprehend and embrace the vision, there is mutual buy-in. Together, they can move forward. Consequently, the leader is now positioned to glide into a role of influence and inspiration.

Vision Maintenance

Maintaining optimum spiritual vision is crucial. Once we are suitably matched to our Designer's eyewear, we must strive to keep them looking like new. Our spiritual lenses should remain free of spots and smears that can affect our focus. Spots and smears may symbolize the marring effects of our gifts if we become distracted. For example, distractions in the form of gifts that you don't possess but are attempting to operate in are like a spot or a smear. We must do whatever it takes to remove these smudges by reattaching to our God-infused spiritual gift, thereby enhancing our spiritual focus.

We must be intentional when it comes to maintaining and enhancing our visual health. The Ultimate Designer, through His Son, Jesus, set the example of how to boost spiritual vision. He engaged in spiritual disciplines such as study, meditation, prayer (solitude and silence), fasting, worship, service, and fellowship with other believers. Likewise, our spiritual vision will be enhanced as we practice the following.

- Study—Read and study God's Word for guidance and direction.

- Meditate—Ponder God's Word to maintain spiritual focus.

- Pray—Commune with God (solitude) and listen to Him (silence).

- Fast—Abstain from food or other distractors for a designated period.

- Worship—Engage in private and corporate worship, which connects us to God.

- Serve—Assist others compassionately, as Jesus did.

- Fellowship—Interact with other believers for encouragement and to equip each other for service.

As we engage in these maintenance practices, we will achieve the Designer's fashionable look. In addition, our vision will be remarkably enhanced, and our spiritual focus will be maximized. We will see objects at any distance, for we will have been fitted with the Ultimate Designer's eyewear. While optometrists utilize digital measurements to ensure an accurate and precise prescription, the Ultimate Designer operates with a precision that is unmatchable.

Finally, the gift of leadership is a unique adornment assigned by the Holy Spirit. Once believers receive confirmation of this gift, they will seek to achieve clearer vision through the lens of the cross. Jesus, the Anointed One, will be their focal point and example as they exercise this spiritual gift in love and faithfulness. As they fully trust God, the Ultimate Designer, and wear the lenses of leadership, they will minister with a touch of grace. The Holy Spirit has assigned the eyewear of leadership to enhance spiritual vision by adding or subtracting focusing power to the lives of gifted believers. I have shared several guarantees that accompany this corrective remedy. The spiritual lenses of leadership prescribed by the Holy Spirit are:

- Progressive—they enable wearers to see both near and far.

- Shatterproof—they are reliable and unbreakable.

- Impact-resistant—they withstand any opposing or colliding force.

- Scratch-resistant—they cannot be scratched or damaged

In addition, the frames attached to these spiritual lenses have the following features:

- Spring-loaded—they are less likely to be bent or warped

- Silicone Nose Pads—they prevent the eyeglasses from slipping

- Straps—they hold the glasses firmly in place

Congratulations! You have experienced spiritual eyesight through the lenses of leadership. Your knowledge and appreciation of this gift have been expanded. Since it is imperative that you identify, cultivate, and operate in your assigned gifts (1 Pet. 4:10; 1 Cor. 12 and 14), I encourage you to prayerfully confirm and validate your divine endowment. Discovering and confirming your spiritual gifts will help you remain in your ministry lane, thereby avoiding a head-on collision.

Has it become apparent that leadership is your gifting? If so, praise the Lord for adorning you with such a precious ornament—the gift of leadership. I encourage you to continue to seek the Lord as you strive to cultivate and operate in this divine gift. If you need further guidance in identifying your spiritual gift, prayerfully navigate through the next chapters. Continue to review the remaining motivational gifts of the Spirit for identification and confirmation.

The Gifted Believer's Prayer:

Almighty God, how excellent is your name in all the earth. As I declare your greatness, adoration and praise flows from my heart and echoes from my lips. Lord, I acknowledge my shortcomings and approach you with a repentant spirit. Forgive my trespasses as I forgive those who have trespassed against me. Thank you for infusing me with the gift of leadership. I treasure your choice in this gifting, for you can make no mistake. Your Word always produces fruit, and it will accomplish all that you have declared. As I embrace this gift, infuse me with divine strength and power. My desire is to provide solid leadership to the body of believers with constant diligence. Thank you for your grace. I offer this prayer in the name of Jesus. Amen.

CHAPTER 7

THROUGH THE LENSES OF MERCY

"IF IT IS TO SHOW MERCY, DO IT CHEERFULLY." ~ ROMANS 12:8 (NIV)

Just as prescriptive lenses improve physical vision, the motivational spiritual gifts of Romans 12 enhance our spiritual vision. Each gift functions like a pair of lenses, sharpening our spiritual focus as we serve others in the body of Christ. These gifts are frequently cited as "motivational gifts" because they are practical in nature and describe the inner motivations of gifted believers. Each believer has inherent motivational tendencies that drive the way he or she responds to various circumstances. The spiritual gifts affect how we see life and respond to the needs around us. As the Ultimate Designer, the Holy Spirit infuses each of us with a customized spiritual gift, which allows us to see people and circumstances through a specific set of lenses that remedy our impaired vision.

The Designer's Eyewear promotes godly and righteous living as a prerequisite for operating in the seven areas of spiritual giftedness. In the prelude to Romans 12, the apostle Paul urged the church in Rome to present their bodies as living sacrifices (12:1–2). He went on to urge them to offer humble service in the body of Christ (12:3). In addition, regenerated believers will also possess the fruit of the Spirit of Galatians 5:22–23—love, joy, peace, longsuffering, gentleness, goodness, faith, meekness, and temperance. Accordingly, as Spirit-filled believers wear the Designer's prescriptive lenses or spiritual eyewear, their vision will align more closely with how God views the world.

This book is based on the presumption that love conquers all. Immediately following the list of spiritual gifts, the apostle Paul further challenged the church to translate love into action (Rom. 12:9–21). He emphasized the sincerity, devotion, zeal, fervor, joy, compassion, and empathy demonstrated through genuine love. True disciples of Christ will exhibit love when operating in their spiritual giftedness. The supremacy of love always overrules the desire to disrupt the flow of the church's mission. We should never allow spiritual giftings to supersede Christian character. On the contrary, character should rise to the forefront while the gifting lags slightly. It is futile to attempt to exercise a spiritual gift without blending it with genuine affection and consideration of others. The apostle Paul eloquently expresses this spiritual truth in 1 Corinthians 13:1 (NIV): "If I speak in the tongues of men and angels, but do not have love, I am only a resounding gong or a clanging cymbal." *The Designer's Eyewear* is written with the notion that each spiritual gift is implemented and aligned with God's Word.

Gift Overview

The Ultimate Designer, God Almighty, is dedicated to presenting various options and exclusives in designer eyewear just for you. In this chapter, I present the seventh and final motivational spiritual gift of Romans 12, the gift of mercy. As with the other spiritual gifts, the Holy Spirit assigns this gift to certain believers. This gift is a supernatural endowment where one demonstrates sympathy and compassion to those who are suffering, blended with exceeding joy in meeting their needs. People with the gift of mercy are sensitive to the emotional and spiritual needs of others. They operate without judging the recipients of their loving deeds. The mercy-giver's utmost desire is to refresh the souls of individuals in distress.

Mercy-givers demonstrate an abiding empathy toward those who are suffering or afflicted. They empathize with comforting words and selfless deeds. Such believers are drawn to individuals who are experiencing trials and difficulties. Mercy-givers are ready and willing to assist the needy over an extended period. Their overwhelming concern for the welfare of the afflicted is indescribable, to say the least. Mercy-givers burn with compassion and a deep desire to lift the burdens of the downtrodden and to help them re-build their lives. These deep empathetic emotions propel mercy-givers to perform tangible acts of kindness. The gift of mercy is one of the most underrated of the seven motivational gifts. In a world where self-absorption is increasing, few people are willing to submit to a role that requires assisting or enabling others. Instead, numerous individuals, including Christians, have embarked on an endless quest to avoid lending aid to the oppressed.

There are misconceptions associated with the gift of mercy. One misbelief is that mercy-givers are "spineless" and "gutless" Christians. This misconception is far from the truth, as established by the following points. Instead of adopting this falsehood, let us focus on kindness vs. spinelessness. Demonstrating genuine compassion and empathy does not equate to being feeble, ineffectual, or weak. After all, didn't Jesus model compassion and empathy? Scripture describes Him as the Lion *and* the Lamb (Rev. 5:5–6, KJV). These two descriptions seem contradictory, but they are not. Those with lion-like personalities gravitate toward "Jesus the Lion," while others with lamb-like personalities identify with "Jesus the Lamb." Jesus displayed strength and meekness. Likewise, spiritually gifted mercy-givers, under the influence of the Holy Spirit, are both strong and meek. Doctrinally speaking, Jesus is both the conquering Lion of the tribe of Judah and the Lamb who was slain. As the Lion of Judah, He fulfilled the prophecy of Genesis 49:9 and is the Messiah who would come from the tribe of Judah. As the Lamb of God, He is the perfect and ultimate sacrifice for sin. What beautiful descriptions of the two aspects of the nature of Christ.

Gifted mercy-givers operate under the power of the Holy Spirit in strength and meekness. They stand on the pillars of scripture (particularly Rom. 12:10–13) as they offer love, compassion, and empathy to those who are distressed. Mercy-givers exhibit courage as they honor others above themselves while responding with a strong spiritual fervor in service to the Lord. Mercy-givers are motivated to edify the body of Christ through their loving and merciful deeds. God honors such a bold and courageous call to duty. All spiritual gifts, qualifications for office, and appointments, are determined by the Holy Spirit, who is intelligent, authoritative and intentional. Therefore, He does not specialize in mishaps, nor does He endow believers with second-rate gifts. All spiritual gifts add value to the body of Christ as believers are guided by God's Spirit.

Conclusively, the gift of mercy cannot be aligned with being spineless or gutless. As the Holy Spirit infuses believers with spiritual gifts, they become endowed with a unique skill set that enables them to minister wholeheartedly. As noted in a previous chapter, Henry T. Blackaby says, "God does not call the qualified, but He qualifies the called." Gifted mercy-givers are qualified to serve the body of Christ as God's Spirit converts their behavioral tendencies, talents, skills, and special abilities into a supernatural manifestation of greatness.

Another misguided view is that Christians who frequently exhibit sympathy possess the gift of mercy. This is far from the truth. Scripture reveals that all Christians are called to be merciful. As God extends mercy toward us, He expects us to extend this act toward others as well. (cf. Matt. 18: 33; Eph. 2:4–6). Gifted mercy-givers, however, are divinely endowed—set apart from other believers. The Holy Spirit equips them with a unique ability to recognize a need and to respond swiftly and cheerfully, administering both spiritual and emotional assistance. One of the qualities that distinguishes spiritually gifted mercy-givers from other believers is their ability to demonstrate empathy. Sometimes we confuse empathy with its closely related cousin, sympathy. Although the two qualities are intricately linked, they are distinct. While many Christians demonstrate sympathy toward others, not all display empathy. Sympathy involves feeling sorrow or pity for the hardships of another person. Empathy requires that we go a step further. It is "the ability to sense other people's emotions, coupled with the ability to imagine what someone else might be thinking or feeling."[29] Empathetic believers not only feel sympathetic toward those in distress, they also emotionally place themselves in the other person's shoes. Once they enter this emotional arena, empathetic believers become driven to lift the burdens of those in distress and to help them rebuild their lives. These deep empathetic emotions propel mercy-givers to perform tangible acts of kindness.

While sympathy and empathy are often used interchangeably, they differ greatly in their meanings. There is no empathy without sympathy, but it is possible to display sympathy without empathy. Indeed, empathy is the catalyst that steers the sympathetic heart toward action. Mercy-givers demonstrate an abiding awareness of empathy toward those who are suffering or afflicted. Those with this gift are drawn to individuals who are experiencing trials and difficulties. Mercy-givers burn with a combination of sympathy and empathy to lift heavy hearts. They "weep with those who weep"; consequently, they readily "rejoice with those who rejoice" (Rom. 12:15). When others overlook the needs of those who are oppressed, a mercy-giver's sharp spiritual discernment draws him or her to the need. When sympathy is blended with empathy, mercy is churned, and tangible results flow in abundance. True mercy-givers demonstrate sympathy and empathy.

As we continue to seek knowledge and clarity through scripture and prayer, the Holy Spirit will illuminate our thinking and steer us away from such misconceptions.

Mercy in the New Testament

Mercy is demonstrated throughout the New Testament. Here are some examples.

---

29 "What is Empathy?", *Greater Good Magazine,* last visited April 29, 2020, www.greatergood.berkeley.edu/topic/empathy/definition.

- Jesus demonstrated mercy to the poor and needy. (Ps. 72:13, KJV)

- God blesses those who are merciful (Matt. 5:7, KJV)

- Jesus had compassion on the crowd (Mk. 6:34, KJV)

- The good Samaritan demonstrates mercy (Lk. 10:33–37, KJV)

- God, our Savior, saved us according to His own mercy (Tit. 3:4–5)

- God described as being rich in mercy (Eph. 2:4–5)

The gift of mercy, designed for edifying the body of Christ, is also referenced in Romans 12:8 (KJV).

The greatest mercy-giver of all time is our Lord and Savior, Jesus. His demonstration of mercy while on earth was strikingly impacting. The entire gospel—the life, death, burial, and resurrection of Christ—reflects His countless acts of mercy and service to humankind. Jesus's unmatchable compassion and empathy is illustrated in the following chart.

Jesus's Compassion and Empathy	Scripture Reference
Drove Him to the bedsides of the afflicted	Matthew 8:14–15; Luke 7:1–10, 7:11–17; Mark 5:21–24, 35–43
Drew Him to encounter and defeat wicked demonic spirits	Mark 1:21–27; Matthew 8:28–33, Mark 7:24–30; Luke 9:37–43

Jesus's Compassion and Empathy	Scripture Reference
Compelled Him to "wine and dine" with sinners	Matthew 9:10–17; Mark 2:13–17; Luke 5:29–39
Steered Him into the company of outcasts	Matthew 8:1–4; Mark 1:41; Luke 17:11–19
Impelled Him to resuscitate the dead and to stop a funeral processional	Matthew 9:18, 23–26; John 11:38–44, Luke 7:11–17
Caused Him to break through racial barriers	Corinthians 12:13; Colossians 3:11; Ephesians 2:11–22; James 2:9; Revelation 7:9–10
Led Him to feed thousands with what many would consider a "poor person's" meal	Matthew 14:13–21; Mark 6:31–44, 8:1–13; John 6:1–14

Jesus's ultimate demonstration of mercy, however, took place in a bizarre setting. This episode occurred at a spot outside of Jerusalem called Golgotha, which in Aramaic means "place of the skull." At that site, also known as Calvary, the Crucifixion took place. Jesus was tortured and executed by being nailed to a cross. The Son of God was crucified alongside two thieves with the charge of claiming to be "King of the Jews." Jesus's family and friends watched Him suffer in agony on the cross, suffering for our sake. On Calvary, Jesus, the Savior of humankind, was forsaken by God and cried with a loud voice, "Eli, Eli, lama sabachthani," meaning "My God, my God, why hast thou forsaken me?" (Matt. 27:46, KJV). He was then given vinegar to wet His lips, and a spear was thrust into His side. It was at that dreary site that the Roman soldiers divided Jesus's clothes before He bowed His head and died. What an unmatchable demonstration of mercy, where compassion and empathy are in full view. Jesus, the sacrificial Lamb, gave His life in exchange for ours. It is said that "He came to pay a debt He did not owe, because we owed a debt we could not pay." The King of Kings laid down His life that we might obtain life. He reiterates this in John 10:10b (KJV), "I am come that they might have life, and that they might have it more abundantly."

Jesus, the ultimate Mercy-giver, left us a blueprint for ministering, centered upon a passion to exhibit mercy to those whose souls need refreshing. We all need inspiration and reinforcement for serving in the body of Christ. Not all of us are gifted as mercy-givers, but we can all demonstrate compassion. Whether we volunteer to seek shelter for the homeless or feed those who are starving, we need to emulate our Savior by showing pity to those in distress.

Motivational Tendencies

The seven motivational gifts of Romans 12 are practical in nature and describe the inner motivations of Christian servants. These spiritual gifts produce certain motivating or influencing tendencies that drive how we relate to others and to our surroundings. The Holy Spirit infuses every believer with qualities that shape their overall perspective on life. Because of this, we find ourselves acting out specific inborn tendencies. This is an indication of our Creator's unique craftsmanship.

People gifted in mercy are motivated to comfort those who are experiencing trials and difficulties. They are endowed with a long-suffering spirit accompanied by a huge lump of patience.

When other believers in the body of Christ fail to meet the needs of those who are in want, mercy-givers step up to the plate. They will not abandon those who are afflicted. Instead, mercy-givers offer support and assistance until the burden is lifted. Mercy-givers lean wholeheartedly on Galatians 6:2 (NIV), which urges us to "bear one another's burdens." This is not always accomplished with ease. Mercy can be costly, but Jesus offers an inspirational declaration in Matthew 5:7 (NIV): "Blessed are the merciful, for they will be shown mercy." As we extend mercy to others, mercy is reciprocated. This is certainly an awe-inspiring promise.

Have you been endowed with the gift of mercy? Are you drawn to people who are suffering or are in distress? Does helping the sick, needy, disabled, and the elderly excite you? Do people attempt to seek you out when they are having difficulties? Do you find yourself interested in ministries that involve things like job placement, food pantries, shelters, and assisted living homes?

As you continue in your quest to identify and confirm your gift, determine whether these motivational tendencies match your own. If they do, you are already reaping the joy that comes with such a beautiful ornament—the gift of mercy. If the attributes listed do not reflect your motivational tendencies, we encourage you to continue seeking the Lord in the validation of your spiritual gift.

Let us observe what it is like to view people and circumstances through the lenses of a mercy-giver. The following list provides descriptions common to those who are equipped with this gift.

- Mercy-givers have a divine ability to sense hurt and respond to it with compassion and empathy.

- Mercy-givers are attracted to people who are in misery; they embrace those that most people tend to disregard.

- Mercy-givers are kind and gentle in character; they operate without judging.

- Mercy-givers are loyal and trustworthy friends and react harshly toward anyone who attacks their friends.

- Mercy-givers have a need for commitment in a close friendship. This may cause them to monopolize the time and attention of others. When they experience disappointment in one friendship, mercy-givers tend to place greater demands on new friendships. However, they do not have a high tolerance for friends who manifest a critical spirit.

- Mercy-givers sense and reflect the spiritual and emotional atmosphere around them. Whereas prophets, leaders, and teachers often project their attitudes to others, individuals who have the gifts of mercy and exhortation (encouragement) are more likely to sense how others are feeling.

- Most mercy-givers desire to feel needed. Believers with this gift must reach out and get involved, or their mercy will turn inward, resulting in an introspective focus that concentrates on their own hurts or fears.[30]

- Mercy-givers may display hypersensitivity, the act of being abnormally or excessively sensitive to tragic news. They tend to refrain from reading or viewing media

---

30 See more from the Institute in Basic Life Principles (https://iblp.org).

coverage that features violent or traumatic stories. This type of news consumption makes mercy-givers stressed out and may cause feelings of anxiety, fatigue, or a loss of sleep.

- Mercy-givers are drawn to other sensitive individuals.

- Mercy-givers tend to release their feelings through prayer.

- Mercy-givers have a sharp sense of discernment. They have a God-given ability to sense a person's spirit or the atmosphere among a group of people. They recognize the feelings that may be at work in others' minds and hearts. When mercy-givers walk in the Spirit, this gift equips them to reach out to people who are suffering but who would likely be reluctant to tell others about their needs.

- Mercy-givers frequently consider the following areas of concentration when considering college majors: health sciences, medicine, psychology, social work, and sociology.

- Mercy-givers are good listeners and feel the need to support and assist others.

- Mercy-givers can be indecisive, ruffled by their strong emotions.

- Mercy-givers may become rescuers of those who do not need to be rescued. They easily allow others to become dependent on them when the individuals should be dependent on God.[31]

---

31 For more on this, see the Institute of Basic Life Principles (www.iblp.org).

- A mercy-giver's warmth can be falsely interpreted as personal, intimate affection. Mercy givers must learn to temper their demonstration of affections based on the mindsets of those to whom they are ministering. If they fail to do this, both parties may be led into temptation.

- Mercy-givers have a difficult time being firm because they do not wish to offend others. They must realize that greater hurt and offenses will occur if they fail to be decisive. When in positions of leadership, mercy-givers tend to avoid necessary disciplinary action. As a result, the person who should have been disciplined is not brought to repentance, others react to their dismissive leadership, and more conflicts develop.

- Because mercy-givers try to avoid conflict, they often avoid confrontation that is needed. Mercy-givers would rather hide from or ignore their enemies than confront them, even when they are in a position of authority. Delaying the inevitable always leads to more trouble for everyone.

- Mercy-givers can be introspective. Because they are sensitive to hurts, it is easy for them to become overly sensitive to their own emotional pain. If a mercy-giver falls into this trap, he or she will wallow in past offenses, cling to past bitterness, and dwell on past mistakes or sins.

- It is common for mercy-givers to develop a poor self-image since they tend to be introspective and remain acutely aware of their own failures. The longer that mercy-givers dwell on their failures, the more worthless and wicked they feel. Mercy-givers also tend to be worriers as a result of focusing on their own failures.

- Mercy-givers often lean on emotions rather than reason. Because those with the gift of mercy are so sensitive, they are prone to basing their decisions on emotions rather than on principles. Their subjective reasoning can easily cause them to reject biblical doctrines that seem harsh.

- Mercy-givers cut off insensitive people. They quickly recognize and react to people whose words and actions reflect insensitivity to the feelings of others. Rather than trying to help insensitive people, mercy-givers might cut off fellowship with them.

- Mercy-givers often suppress their emotions when wronged by others. Because of their sensitivity to other people's feelings, they are cautious when it comes to rebuking those who have offended them.

- Mercy-givers have an exceptional ability to discern between genuine unconditional love and expressions of love that are insincere or hypocritical. They are overly sensitive to statements and actions that may hurt others.

In conclusion, a mercy-giver's basic motivation is to demonstrate sympathy and compassion to those who are suffering. They experience ultimate fulfillment as opportunities to meet emotional and spiritual needs are presented. Few moments are more gratifying for mercy-givers than performing selfless deeds that refresh the souls of others. Mercy-givers extend their hearts to support the ministry while bringing glory and honor to our Lord and Savior.

God has equipped each believer with at least one tailor-made gift that matches his or her purpose and destiny. Your entire personality, including your motivations and tendencies, bear the imprint of your gift. If you have the gift of mercy, you will see yourself in the description that follows.

3 C's—Characteristics, Challenges, and Choices

While each person in the body of Christ is unique, it is not unusual for those who operate in the same motivational gift to demonstrate common characteristics, to experience common challenges, and to serve in similar choices, or capacities in ministry.

Characteristics

While everyone in the body of Christ is unique, a believer who operates in the gift of mercy may possess several of the following characteristics.

- Has a divine ability to sense emotional pain

- Exhibits sympathy *and* empathy

- Is drawn to people in distress

- Is sensitive to the needs of those who are hurting

- Is sensitive to statements and actions that may hurt others

- Is kindhearted, patient and considerate

- Is extremely loyal and trustworthy

- Is overprotective of family members and friends

- Has a need for commitment in close friendships

- Is able to discern when people are hurting

- Avoids confrontation and controversy

- Suppresses emotional pain

- Is nonjudgmental of others

- Is a good listener

- Is a peacemaker

Although each person's behavior will vary according to factors such as age, gender, culture, environment, background, temperament, and experiences, it is common for those who have the motivational gift of mercy to demonstrate these characteristics.

Challenges

While everyone in the body of Christ is unique, a believer who operates in the gift of mercy may encounter some of the following challenges.

- Displays hypersensitivity

- Is frequently indecisive

- Is easily offended

- Can be easily taken advantage of

- Has difficulty speaking the truth firmly

- Has difficulty correcting people in error

- Is sometimes devalued

- Is mistaken as weak or "spineless"

- Judges primarily according to feelings

We need to acknowledge all of these challenges and pray diligently to overcome them. As we minister, God's purpose for spiritual gifts must remain in the forefront. He establishes a standard where spiritual gifts can operate in excellence. When we lean toward a carnal focus, Christ's ministry is compromised, which may lead others to discredit the gifts and bypass the benefits they provide. As we stand on the pillar of Philippians 4:13, we can overcome all challenges through Christ, who gives us strength.

Choices (Areas of Service):

While this list is not comprehensive, it can be used as a guide for directing those who are passionate about identifying and operating in their area of spiritual giftedness. The chart below provides the following: 1) suggested positions or areas of service, 2) descriptions of the positions or areas of service, 3) abilities and best personality traits for each position, and 4) the type of ministry or the specific group for whom the person is passionate about serving.[32]

"YOUR GIFT IS GOD'S GIFT TO YOU; WHAT YOU DO WITH IT IS YOUR GIFT TO GOD." ~ UNKNOWN

---

32 Gilbert and Spear, 2002.

Ministry Opportunities: Mercy

Position	Description	Characteristics	Passionate About:
Pantry Organizer	Organizes and maintains the supply of clothing and nonperishable food for benevolent use	*Abilities:* Good organizational skills; self-motivated; capable of working alone but can work well with others. *Personality Traits:* Compassionate and dependable	Organizing things and helping those in need
Prayer Leader	Responsible for organizing and facilitating fervent prayer sessions	*Abilities:* Good organizational and communication skills *Personality Traits:* Compassionate, serious, discreet, and dependable	Praying and emphasizing the power of prayer; encouraging spiritual growth

Senior Care Leader	Provides leadership to a group that expresses Christian love and concern to a group of senior adults through maintaining regular contact and encouragement	*Abilities:* Compassionate, accessible; able to write and mail brief notes and cards *Personality Traits:* Compassionate, consistent, and dependable	Physical, emotional, and spiritual well-being of fellow Christians

This chart serves as a guide to help those with the gift of mercy identify opportunities for serving. Here are other areas of service for ministering in the gift of mercy.

- Counseling

- Emergency shelter

- Food and clothing distribution

- Visitation of the sick and shut-in

- Support groups

Other influencing factors drive a person's ability to minister, including age, level of spiritual maturity, and overall health (physical and emotional). I recommend that you collaborate with local church leadership to develop your passions in ministry. Your spiritual advisors can assist you in selecting suitable options that are readily available within your local church.

In summary, believers gifted in mercy are motivated by the urgency to demonstrate sympathy and empathy to those who are suffering. Now that you've experienced what life looks like through the lenses of mercy, you can develop a deeper appreciation for this gift.

Vision Enhancement

The motivational gifts function like a pair of eyeglasses, maximizing our spiritual vision. The gifts affect how we see life and respond to the needs around us. While prescriptive lenses correct or improve physical eyesight, these seven gifts alter or readjust spiritual sight. Like corrective lenses, as we "wear" these gifts, they serve as a remedy for impaired spiritual vision. They also influence our ability to focus on serving the body of Christ. To enhance physical vision, we must be willing to seek assistance in correcting our defective eyesight. The same is true of our spiritual vision. Consider physical nearsightedness and farsightedness. These are two common defects that can improve with proper intervention. Spiritual gifts can do the same thing for our spiritual vision.

- People who are spiritually nearsighted lack foresight and can only judge what is in front of them. Since such people are short-sighted, they cannot readily see distant images, which appear blurry. Visual accuracy is limited to only what is up close—the obvious.

- Spiritually farsighted individuals, on the other hand, can clearly see distant images, but objects that are in front of them appear blurry. Farsighted people can only judge images at a great distance.

Both visual impairments, nearsightedness and farsightedness, require prescriptive lenses for visual enhancement. It is amazing how these lenses help remedy both defects and improve overall vison. Likewise, if our spiritual eyesight is defective, we must be willing to receive the remedy that the Holy Spirit prescribes in the form of spiritual gifts.

Those who operate in the motivational gifts of the Spirit must clearly see people and circumstances through the lenses of their designated gifts. If we are to serve others in the body of Christ in an effective manner, our ability to focus on spiritual matters cannot be impaired. Believers who are spiritually nearsighted lack discretion in the things of God and cannot see the big picture. They are only capable of judging what is in front of them—the obvious. To nearsighted believers, any consideration outside of their apparent reach seems blurry. On the other hand, Christians who are spiritually farsighted often overlook what is directly in front of them.

In these instances, defective vision represents believers who misrepresent or abuse their spiritual gift(s), operating outside of their divine scope. Here is good news: both visual defects can be remedied. Almighty God, the Ultimate Designer, has provided corrective spiritual lenses that supersede those of any earthly optometrist.

Correcting Nearsightedness in Mercy Giving

Mercy-givers must be careful of becoming spiritually nearsighted and only judging what is in front of them. Here, nearsightedness symbolizes mercy-givers promoting their personal agenda or leaning toward their personal weaknesses, i.e., the challenges detailed in the previous section. Farsightedness, on the other hand, represents a mercy-giver's inability to see the big picture. Mercy-givers must not become short-sighted or be steered primarily by their emotions. Instead, they must extend their spiritual vision into the distance by following the Holy Spirit's leading. In addition, they must exercise spiritual discretion while refraining from rationalizing ungodly conduct.

Mercy-givers who occupy positions of leadership manifest nearsightedness when they fail to implement corrective discipline, as required. Mercy-givers tend to avoid conflict. It is extremely challenging for such believers to assume leadership roles that require correcting those who are in error. When a follower fails to conduct himself of herself in a godly manner, or when someone fails to comply with the church's rules or regulations, rather than confronting the individual in question, mercy-givers tend to delay implementing correction. They begin to rationalize the misbehavior based on wishful thinking. They may even offer excuses for the wrongdoer's misdeeds. Mercy-givers embrace the notion that, eventually, the violator will realize the error of his or her ways and turn full circle. On the contrary, delaying the inevitable will only fuel this fiery misconduct and spark an explosive blaze. This sweltering fire can prove to be very detrimental to the body of Christ.

In this instance, mercy-givers are experiencing nearsightedness. They can only see what is right in front of them and are reluctant to implement corrective action. Mercy-givers shy away from offending the person or people in question. They are hesitant about speaking firmly against any individual. However, mercy-givers must realize that greater hurt and damage will occur if they fail to take a righteous stand. Mercy-givers must comprehend that their position of inactivity, when action or activity is warranted, can be just as detrimental as performing an activity when inaction is justifiable. Their failure to discipline their subordinates may yield negative consequences.

When mercy-givers in leadership fail to correct misbehavior, onlookers begin to express disdain for the leader. Rather than valuing their supportive role, others may characterize mercy-givers as ineffective or cowardly leaders. As a result, the mercy-giver's credibility may diminish, and he or she could lose the confidence of other followers. This may result in a contentious or hostile environment that is not conducive to effective ministry. When this happens, a deed that was intended to be spiritually fruitful becomes tainted and unfruitful. Consequently, the misbehavior goes uncorrected, and issues and challenges persist, causing further chaos, dissention, and emotional upheaval.

When mercy-givers in leadership fail to implement corrective discipline, the guilty party is denied the opportunity to come to repentance. Such people are robbed of their chance for spiritual renewal—to repent and turn from their wrongdoing. Leaders who operate in mercy giving are firm advocates of Romans 15:1 (NIV), "We who are strong ought to bear with the failings of the weak and not to please ourselves." Those who are strong in the faith should show sympathy and consideration for weaker brothers and sisters in Christ. Such acts of kindness should not be limited to benevolent acts only; they must also include empowering others to restore broken relationships with God. When in leadership, a mercy-giver's chief objective should not be to please himself or herself by yielding to his or her emotions. Instead, mercy-givers must base their decisions on the infallible Word of God. They must never accommodate ungodly conduct at any price; instead, they should continually create opportunities to refresh the souls of others through godly repentance.

Mercy-givers who fail to correct offenders are in violation of obedience to God's Word. By failing to carry out their responsibilities as spiritual leaders, mercy-givers can become entangled in a web of deception. By focusing on sparing the feelings of others, they run the risk of compromising their relationship with God. Mercy-givers must be careful that their emotional reasoning does not steer them into rejecting biblical truths, even though those truths may seem harsh.

Because mercy-givers have a strong disdain for offending others, they tend to avoid confrontations. Their feelings of sensitivity toward others may also override their ability to make sound judgments as leaders. They often base their decisions on emotions as opposed to principles. When this occurs, their positive image may be overridden by their failure to act. Again, a mercy-giver's personal feelings may cause them to reject biblical truths that they interpret as too strict.

As spiritually mature leaders gifted in mercy, mercy-givers set elevated standards of excellence for godly behavior. They prayerfully steer their followers from disorder to order—from disorganization to organization. Many times, this transformation can only be achieved as followers are held accountable of their actions. In 1 Samuel 2:12–36, it is evident that laxness in discipline results in grief. Eli, a father and high priest in ancient Israel, was well-versed in God's law. When his sons committed ungodly acts, including robbing God in offerings, mistreating other Israelites, and committing acts of immorality with women who served at the tabernacle, Eli failed to take disciplinary action. Instead of removing his sons from their priestly office and ejecting them from serving in the sanctuary, Eli dismissed their sinful behavior. Eventually, his sons were killed in battle, and Eli, upon hearing the report, fell backward off his seat by the gate and broke his neck (1 Sam. 4:10, 11, and 18). The example of Eli's laxness in disciplining his sons further substantiates that any abuse of our position as servants of God for selfish gain will bring God's judgement upon us.

Our visual accuracy should go beyond the close and obvious—nearsightedness—and extend to distant images. It is evident that mercy-givers see what is right in front of them, but distant objects are often blurry. They are unable to focus on the big picture—their obligation to obey and to please God. People with the gift of mercy can see beyond the obvious by extending their vision into the distance. All believers must correct defective vision, spiritual nearsightedness, and strive to envision distant objects, symbolic of overcoming challenges associated with our spiritual gift(s).

Correcting Farsightedness in Mercy Giving

Mercy-givers must also be careful of becoming spiritually farsighted. Focusing primarily on distant images or the big picture will cause them to miss what is directly in front of them. Here, farsightedness represents a mercy-giver's inherent desire to lift another's burden through close contact and personal bonding.

Mercy-givers may be driven only to see images in the distance—the end results of that special personal connection—without considering what's right in front of them: the recipient's weak and deceptive nature. A mercy-giver's friendliness and warmth can also be falsely interpreted as personal, intimate affection. They must be careful to temper their demonstration of affection, particularly with the opposite sex, based on the mindset of those to whom they are assisting. If they fail to do so, both parties may be led into a deep sea of temptation.

Mercy-givers possess a unique quality that shapes their overall perspective. They are unconsciously driven by a passion to comfort those in misery. As they operate in this mode, this dominant motivational tendency may dull their judgment. As a result, they fail to notice the recipient's character flaws. Mercy-givers are so consumed with refreshing the souls of the distressed that they overlook what appears to be a blemish. While a blemish is only a small mark or flaw, it has the potential to spread and cause great harm. The appearance of a seemingly tiny blemish represents negative traits, such as selfishness, greed, envy, malice, or excessive anger. These things can transform into such vices as sexual perversion, drunkenness, gambling, or prostitution. Mercy-givers must be cautious when extending comforting words and performing benevolent deeds. Though mercy-givers have good intentions, some people are quick to swindle, defraud, and exploit kind people. These negative character traits may appear as tiny blemishes at first; however, they can become more pronounced.

On occasion, mercy-givers may be tricked into providing comfort to a swindler. Their quest to uplift and refresh souls may cause them to overlook certain character flaws. However, when mercy-givers prayerfully operate under the Holy Spirit's influence, their discernment is sharpened. Then and only then are they able to extend spiritual comfort in words and deeds. When mercy-givers walk in the Spirit, this gift equips them to reach out to people who are suffering but who are unlikely to defraud them.

Again, mercy-givers must exercise extreme caution when bonding with the opposite sex. It is noteworthy to recall the craftiness of Satan, the trickster. He frequently designs opportunities to trap gifted believers. Unlike God, the devil does not flow in originality or creativity. He merely duplicates the same rustic methods time and again. It is not surprising when a cunning and crafty con artist approaches mercy-givers with a legitimate need. This is indicative of the enemy's crafty style. Therefore, gifted believers must be careful to temper their demonstrations of affection, specifically with the opposite sex.

Mercy-givers must also avoid becoming spiritually farsighted—seeing only images in the distance, the big picture. In this illustration, a mercy-giver's focus is on demonstrating compassion to the suffering party. He or she is filled with immeasurable joy in meeting this need and operates without judging the recipients of his or her deeds. Mercy-givers often rescue those who do not need to be rescued solely by people. They must shift the recipient's dependence from people to total dependence on God. This farsightedness causes the images that are close—the recipient's character flaws—to become blurry. Mercy-givers must correct farsightedness, spiritually defective vision. They must seek the Holy Spirit's guidance in focusing on images that are close, such as pronounced character flaws. When this happens, a mercy-giver's kind deeds prove to be spiritually fruitful.

Vision Maintenance

Maintaining optimum spiritual vision is crucial. Once we are suitably matched to our Designer's eyewear, we must strive to keep them looking like new. Our spiritual lenses should remain free of spots and smears that can affect our focus. Spots and smears may symbolize the marring effects of our gifts if we become distracted. For example, distractions in the form of gifts that you don't possess but are attempting to operate in are like a spot or a smear. We must do whatever it takes to remove these smudges by reattaching to our God-infused spiritual gift, thereby enhancing our spiritual focus.

We must be intentional when it comes to maintaining and enhancing our visual health. The Ultimate Designer, through His Son, Jesus, set the example of how to boost spiritual vision. He engaged in spiritual disciplines such as study, meditation, prayer (solitude and silence), fasting, worship, service, and fellowship with other believers. Likewise, our spiritual vision will be enhanced as we practice the following.

- Study—Read and study God's Word for guidance and direction.

- Meditate—Ponder God's Word to maintain spiritual focus.

- Pray—Commune with God (solitude) and listen to Him (silence).

- Fast—Abstain from food or other distractors for a designated period.

- Worship—Engage in private and corporate worship, which connects us to God.

- Serve—Assist others compassionately, as Jesus did.

- Fellowship—Interact with other believers for encouragement and to equip each other for service.

As we engage in these maintenance practices, we will achieve the Designer's fashionable look. In addition, our vision will be remarkably enhanced, and our spiritual focus will be maximized. We will see objects at any distance, for we will have been fitted with the Ultimate Designer's eyewear. While optometrists utilize digital measurements to ensure an accurate and precise prescription, the Ultimate Designer operates with a precision that is unmatchable.

Finally, the gift of mercy is a unique adornment assigned by the Holy Spirit. Once a believer receives confirmation of this gift, he or she will seek to achieve clearer vision through the lens of the cross. Jesus, the Anointed One, should be our focal point and example as we exercise this spiritual gift in love and faithfulness. As we fully trust God, the Ultimate Designer, and wear the lenses of mercy, we will minister with a touch of grace. The Holy Spirit has assigned the eyewear of mercy to enhance spiritual vision by adding or subtracting focusing power to the lives of gifted believers. I have shared several guarantees that accompany this corrective remedy. The spiritual lenses of mercy giving prescribed by the Holy Spirit are:

- Progressive—they enable us to see both near and far

- Shatterproof—they are reliable and unbreakable

- Impact-resistant—they withstand any opposing or colliding force

- Scratch-resistant—they cannot be scratched or damaged

In addition, the frames attached to these spiritual lenses have the following features:

- Spring-loaded—they are less likely to be bent or warped

- Silicone Nose Pads—they prevent the eyeglasses from slipping

- Straps—they hold the glasses firmly in place

Congratulations! You have experienced spiritual eyesight through the lenses of mercy giving. Your knowledge and appreciation of this gift have been expanded. Since it is imperative that you identify, cultivate, and operate in your assigned gifts (1 Pet. 4:10; 1 Cor. 12 and 14), I encourage you to prayerfully confirm and validate your divine endowment. Discovering and confirming your spiritual gifts will help you remain in your ministry lane, thereby avoiding a head-on collision.

Can you confirm that the act of demonstrating mercy to others is your ministry focus? If so, praise the Lord for adorning you with such a precious ornament—the gift of mercy giving. I encourage you to continue to seek the Lord in the cultivation and operation of your divine gift. If you need further guidance in identifying your gift, prayerfully navigate through the previous chapters in this book, and continue to review all the motivational gifts of the Spirit for identification and confirmation.

The Gifted Believer's Prayer:

Father, I come to you in the name of Jesus. I exalt you and make known to you my adoration and praise. Please forgive my trespasses as I forgive those who have trespassed against me. Almighty God, from the fruit of my lips, I offer thanksgiving to you, for I appreciate this precious gift of mercy giving. I treasure your Word, for it is perfect and complete. As I yield myself to your service of demonstrating compassion and empathy, empower me to overcome all distractions associated with this gift. May all that I perform in your name bring glory and honor to you as I help to refresh the souls of those in distress. Amen.

ABOUT THE AUTHOR

Sonya G. Richardson, an ordained minister, is a spiritual gifts enthusiast who has organized and facilitated numerous workshops across Southeastern United States for nearly two decades. Her mission and mandate include steering believers in their quests to identify and cultivate their spiritual gifts for service in the body of Christ.

Sonya is an effective communicator who approaches her area of expertise through the lens of simplification. She is recognized for her exceptional skills in simplifying topics perceived as complex and communicating information in a way that one can easily comprehend.

Sonya is a transformational leader who holds several ministry offices in the state of Georgia. She completed her undergraduate studies and earned a Bachelor of Science degree in Electrical Engineering at Southern University, Baton Rouge, Louisiana. Professionally, Sonya is an engineer and an emerging leader in the aerospace industry.

She currently resides in Atlanta, Georgia with her husband, a local pastor, four adult children, and four grandchildren.

Find out more about Sonya's book, plans, and goals at www.sonyarichardson.com

Made in the USA
Monee, IL
27 November 2025

36546933R10118